THE BOBBY J SONGBOOK

The Bobby Joe Ebola Songbook

A humor miscellany containing lyrics & guitar chords for over 90 songs from the band's complete discography with illustrations by various artists, photographs, anecdotes, and other bizarre detritus.

Corbett Redford & Dan Abbott

Edited, designed, and cover illustrated by Jason Chandler

Interior illustrated by various artists (see appendix for details)

Photo this page: Flip Cassidy

Published by: Microcosm Publishing, 636 SE 11th Ave., Portland, OR 97214

For a catalog, go to www.microcosmpublishing.com

ISBN 978-1-62106-005-5

This is Microcosm 76124

Distributed by IPG, Chicago and Turnaround, UK

First edition published November 15, 2013

PRINTED IN U.S.A.

Introduction

Welcome, Reader, to the Bobby Joe Ebola Songbook! We hope it brings you a bit of diversion from the drudgery and pain of existence. If we've done it right, you'll have a few chuckles, learn a couple of things you didn't know before, and if you find any of our songs entertaining, you'll have the questionable opportunity to learn and play them for yourself.

If you're wondering who "we" is, we're Dan and Corbett of Bobby Joe Ebola and the Children MacNuggits, an odd little music group we've inflicted on the world since 1995. We met in high school, two geeky misfits stuck in a town called Pinole, CA. Since starting this band we've had some very weird and wonderful adventures; We've traveled the world, run a record label, organized underground festivals, and cheated death countless times, all in the pursuit of making art. Music and art can take you to some unexpected places too, if you let it. This book lays out some of the victories and hilarious missteps we've experienced.

And yet, music was not Plan A. We originally came to songwriting, not because we were particularly skilled or talented musicians, but because music was quicker than film, louder & catchier than poetry, and cheaper than college (Though according to what math we've been able to figure out since then, college probably would have been cheaper). The music is, in some ways, merely a delivery system for our awkward observations and musings. We had grand visions of pop success at the beginning, blissfully ignorant of the music industry, or what we were capable of. We barely knew what DIY meant in 1995; now we feel lucky we've gotten to make this crazy journey as an independent band, on our own two feet, surrounded by friends. OK, four feet. Plus however many feet our friends have.

When we started this band we were just out of high school, and most of our influences and attitudes were rooted in pop culture. We slowly unlearned a lot of misogynistic and small-minded lessons we'd internalized from TV, as we went from goofy suburbanites giggling at boobs to clumsy but earnest social critics. In this book you'll find nearly every song we ever wrote, even songs that sorta make us wince nowadays. We were lucky enough to have rad friends who gently challenged our views, and made us think carefully about what our songs were really saying. It's made us better songwriters, and better people. But we present the whole story to you, warts and all. You can't learn from your history if you cover it up.

A few words on how to use this book: We are not trained musicians, and neither of us read music. This songbook will not teach you how to play every note, nor does it indicate vocal melodies, rhythm, or anything else a serious musician would know about. Most of these simple songs were written on guitar, but if you have basic skill with any instrument, you should be able to learn how to play along with our recordings using the lyrics and chords listed here (Check the Appendix and Discography for more information about our recordings).

We hope that our songbook will inspire you to try writing your own songs and finding your own voice. Music isn't something you need handed down to you by experts; why shouldn't you create the soundtrack to your own life? Don't be afraid to look foolish doing something you enjoy. There's no wrong way to do this. If there was, we might never have even started.

**Dan & Corbett,
May 2013**

ɔɹoʍǝɹoℲ

About 20 miles East of San Francisco, California, the city of Pinole overlooks San Pablo Bay, boasting a quaint, historic downtown and a bowling alley. It's a community that evolved over time from a working-class town into a clumsy suburb as the once-thriving industry there vacated and "Big Boxes" marched in. Most people driving on the I-80 East make a joke about the name of the neighboring town Hercules, blink, and then pass Pinole without noticing.

The only reason I ever go to Pinole is to see Dan and Corbett. Seriously. It's a shithole with more Hometown Buffets than it deserves. I know, because I am from a similar shithole. They once told me there was an abandoned dynamite factory there, somewhere, overgrown with vegetation and radiating sketchy potential. Even that siren call to mischief wasn't enough to drag me out there. But seeing Dan and Corb is.

We originally met as kindred goofballs in the East Bay punk scene. We were all screwing around in the margins of an already marginalized group. If the punks were the rats in the walls, we were the stink bugs.

Being silly in an underground music scene is a double-edged banana peel. Cut your heartfelt lyrics with humor and people don't think you're serious. Cut your jokes with meaning and hecklers cry, "Be funny, clown!" Dan and Corbett found the balance.

At some point "novelty" became a dirty word in music. Uttering that word caused lawns to die and all coolness in a mile radius to wilt like a flower made of limp dongs. Bobby Joe Ebola got shanked with that square peg early on. But they gleefully flew that label high, like a pair of stolen underwear run up a flagpole.

And they kept doing it. Then they stopped doing it. Then they came back and have kept doing it with a vengeance and every god damn resource they have.

The combination of Dan and Corbett's songwriting seems effortless. There is a workmanlike quality to the phrasing and the lyrics, a Johnny Cash level of brevity that tells a sprawling story in the most simple way. The words wink before they stab you. And the dark ideas don't crush you because they rest on musical hooks like pads of sweet cream butter. The weirdness never feels forced because it comes from an honest place. They're both pretty weird. Trust me.

I wouldn't say they wear their heart on their sleeve. I think it's more appropriate to say they tear their hearts from their chest, stretch them all over their body like a baby's onesie and then dance.

What does it all sound like? Imagine a moment between when the air raid sirens call and that famous, final flash of total planetary annihilation.

Everyone runs.

Dan and Corb march toward ground zero and sing.

That's what Bobby Joe Ebola and The Children MacNuggits sound like.

This book is a guide on how to go for broke and break everything.

**Alex Koll,
June 2013**

3

TABLE OF CONTENTS

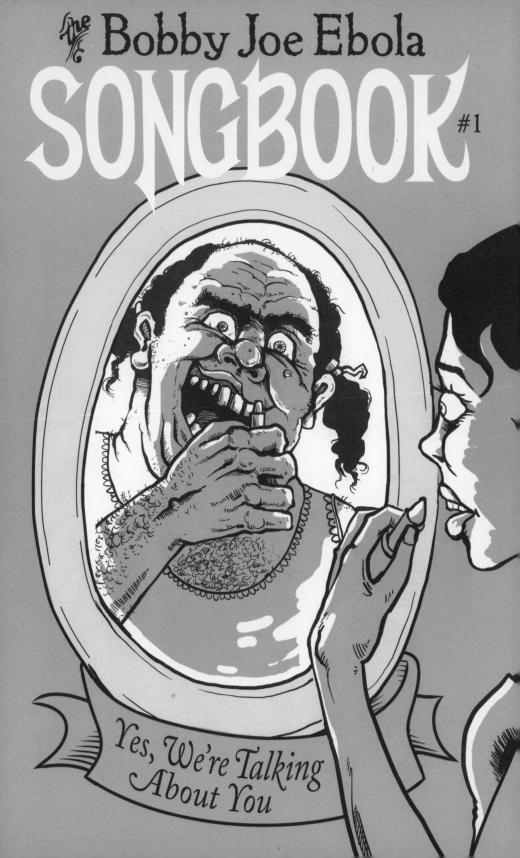

DID YOU KNOW?

At the tender age of 14, Dan won the Jim Morrison Bad Poetry Contest at Fud's Guitar Shop in Alameda, CA. The three drunken judges inexplicably gave him a rusty nail as a prize, and his poem and photo were printed in *Tales of Jerry*, a comic book about Jim Morrison as a randy, poetry-spouting vampire.

WRITERS ~ DAN ABBOTT & CORBETT REDFORD /// EDITOR ~ JASON CHANDLER
CONTRIBUTING ILLUSTRATORS (SEE APPENDIX FOR DETAILS):
M. FOXALL, M. CLEM, W. SMITH, H. MACLEAN, J. NOVAK, B. ZABLACKIS,
J. COTTERILL, C. FORSLEY, P. AGUILERA, P. SORFA, A. WARNER, B. PINKEL,
M. CLOTFELTER, R. Z. RIFFEY, M. PALM, M. O'DRISCOLL, J. ISAACSON

HELLO CRUEL WORLD!

The world is an ugly little place. We are all born radiant fuckers, full of love and truth and so forth. But the world, in its desire to make itself look presentable, brushes the grime from itself onto us. Icky! By the time we can talk, we're soiled by the constant sooty dandruff of tyrannies both large and petty. And this process compels us to shake that same filth off onto something else, anything else. We try to join up, to be pretty or strong or popular or rich. We are eternally at war with ourselves; the public persona, the affable and popular shell, is the source of our self-loathing and melancholy. We are fake, fake charlatans, hypocrites and liars, all of us. We all know it, cry it into our pillow at night or spackle over our self-doubt with industrial strength booze.

As we've said many times, we tried to be normal, but we were never very good at it. As teenagers, when we thought we were blending in at a party, someone would sniff us out; some kid with a bright future would recognize us and it would all end in laughter and stuff in our hair, or blood. Even later, in our adult lives, the jocks and cheerleaders were replaced by shift managers and cops. By then, of course, the feeling was mutual.

As outsiders, we became pretty good at seeing through people's coping mechanisms. We see the masks and what lays behind them, both yours and our own. Some of these observations became the songs in this chapter. It'd be pretty cool if, all at once, we saw the ways we've been twisted and manipulated by society, and all tore off our masks together. But some of 'em are glued on pretty good. So be gentle playing these songs to others, OK?

🎵 Bobby Joe Ebola Songbook #1 ~ TABLE OF CONTENTS

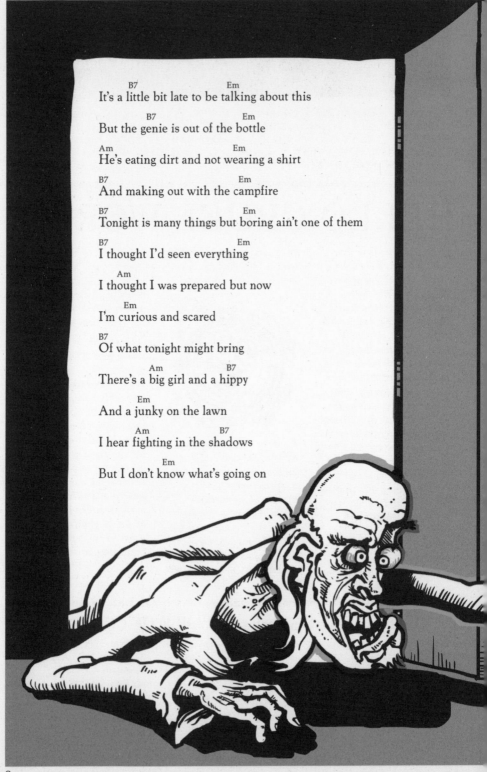

B7   Em
It's a little bit late to be talking about this

B7   Em
But the genie is out of the bottle

Am   Em
He's eating dirt and not wearing a shirt

B7   Em
And making out with the campfire

B7   Em
Tonight is many things but boring ain't one of them

B7   Em
I thought I'd seen everything

    Am
I thought I was prepared but now

    Em
I'm curious and scared

B7
Of what tonight might bring

        Am   B7
There's a big girl and a hippy

        Em
And a junky on the lawn

        Am   B7
I hear fighting in the shadows

        Em
But I don't know what's going on

Am   B7
And the gay dude with the garden

        Em   Am
hasn't done anything wrong

        B7
He's the only voice of reason

        Em   B7 Em
in this song

        B7   Em
I don't want to seem ungrateful

                        B7
and I'm having fun

                        Em
But I'm ready to go to sleep

                Am
We're like the camera crew of COPS

                Em
but there's no way to make it stop

  B7
And we're too drunk to leave

        Am   B7
There's a fat girl with a fat lip

        Em
And two drunk crying dudes

        Am   B7
And the junky's trying to set fire

        Em
to all his bad tattoos

        Am   B7   Em   Am
The hippy claws into the closet trying to break on through
        B7   Em   B7 Em
Like a trainwreck to Narnia

9

ALL MY FRIENDS ARE DRUG FIENDS

    C   F
They don't know nothing about history

    C   G   G7
To them, knowledge is a mystery

    C   F   Fm
They don't know nothing about math

    C   G   C
I wonder if they've ever used a bath

(*Chorus*)

C7
Are they sleeping in their vomit?

D7
Me I'll put my money on it

G   G7   C
All my friends are drug fiends

C7
PCP, smack, dope, and speed,

D7
that's what they say they all need

G   G7   C
All my friends are drug fiends

    C   F
They got a big 'ol jug of Visine

    C   G   G7
Their needles all the time are unclean

    C   F   FM
Their grandma, the woman she ain't flaccid

    C   G   C
They stole her money so they could score some acid

(*Chorus*)

    Am   F
The gutter is what they call their home (their home!)

   Am   F
On the streets drooling they roam (they roam!)

       Am   F
They covet their 40-foot drug pipe

       G
If you cram it with weed, as much as they need.

Do that and they won't gripe

    C   F
They like that heroin in their cocaine

    C   G
They don't have any cells in their brain

    C   F   Fm
To them, the pot laws are a joke

    C   G   C
To them, life's just one big toke

(*Chorus*)

CENSOR THE WORD

WHY DONT WE CENSOR THE WORD 'CUNT?
CENSOR THE WORD 'CUNT'?
CENSOR THE WORD 'CUNT'?

A   F
Ten thousand words is way too many anyway

A#   E A# C# B D G#
Who will miss one word?

A   F
Nobody needs to hear it and some people fear it

         C   B
Because they are upset by cunt juice

(Chorus)

Gm   Cm   Eb   F#
Euphemisms used for jism, shit and seed or stool

   Gm   Cm   Eb   F#
Excuse me while I shit on your seat

       Gm   Cm   Eb F#
And plant my cum in your garden

E   D   D   A
Porn will make you rape, therapy will make you straight

       C   G   A
And the Army makes you feel alright

          C   E
Why don't we censor the word 'cunt'?

C   E   E
Censor the word 'cunt'? Censor the word 'cunt'?

     A   F
I got respect for the cleft of which men are bereft

   A#   E A# C# B D G#
Cos I'm a fissure man

    A   F
I'll snatch your gash in a slit-second splash

   C   B
Cos I am not annoyed by your void

(Chorus)

A   B A# B A# B A# B
I stood on the roof a whole four hours today

 A#   B A# B A# B A# B
This time I'm really really not joking

  A#   B A#   B A# B A# B
I was just two inches from the ledge this time

  A#   B A# B B A# B A#
And I mustered up an actual tear

      Em   Bm
Hell yes I'm depressed, See, I'm a mess

    C   D   C   D Em
And I'm trying to get that sunken thing down

   G   Bm
Here's a test, Do you jest?

    C   D   C D Em
Will he actually blow the whole house down?

    G   Bm
It's a chocolate gun, Somewhere there's a pun

    C D C   D   C   D
I should run to a place where no one knows I'm a liar

A#   A   Dm
I heard my youngest uncle went out like this

  A#   A   Dm
With a yellow peep in his mouth and his thang in his fist

    A#   A   Dm
Acting like an acid casualty with all his body hair shaved

     A#   A   Dm
It must have made for a great cover story

    A#   A   Dm
But mine will sell more records...

IT'S A SMALL WORLD

Corbett once delivered a pizza to John Fogerty of Creedence Clearwater Revival at his mansion in Pinole. He didn't tip. Ironically, Dan and Corbett ended up with his old couch after a friend of theirs bought it at a yard sale Fogerty held. It was upon this very couch where the band wrote dozens of the early BJE songs.

14

PINOLE FACTS

PINOLE WAS THE BEDROOM COMMUNITY FOR WORKERS AT THE NEARBY HERCULES POWDER WORKS FACTORY, WHICH PRODUCED MORE DYNAMITE FOR WORLD WAR I THAN ANY OTHER PLANT IN THE WORLD.

FRESHMAN PHILOSOPHY

F# E B   F#   E   B
I want to be a freshman philosopher, Wear black, stare and look depressed

         F# E B
Complain that I am so unpopular

       F# E   B
And write love songs in a spiral
  notebook

Bm   G
Can't you see the darkness in my soul

     Bm
The French will dig my poems
      G   A
more than Edgar Allen Poe

       E B   F# E B
I want to be...... Freshman Philosophy

F#   E   B
I want to be the Lonely One

F# E   B   F#   E   B
I'll be sad like Robert Smith. Do lots of drugs and listen to Morrisey

F#   E   B
Read about Nietzsche & slash my wrists
Bm   G
Contemplate the limits of reality
Bm   G
How come no one's ever thought

       A
of this but me?
    E B   F#   E B
I want to be...... Freshman Philosophy

F#   E   B
I'm consumed by pain that no one sees

F#   E   B
Kerouac is cool on LSD

F#   E   B
Underline my copy of Dostoyevsky

F#   E   B   F#   E   B
Dress like an extra from Sid and Nancy, Mom and Dad want to test my pee.

    C   Em   F   C
You took me in from the street

              Em
I didn't even say hi to you

    F   G   C
I just went to your fridge to get something to eat

                  Em   F
When you go out to work I make long distance calls

C   Em   F   G
And nail JC Penney panty ads on your walls

                        C   Em F G   C
And you're only renting   you're only renting

              Em   F   C
I'll do your best friend on your brand-new pleather couch

             Em   F
Bring over my boa constrictor, let it play with your pet mouse

C   Em
Take over the remote control,

              F
    watch pro bowling instead of "Friends"

C   Em
And the day of your abortion

    F   G
    was the day that I slept in

C   Em
Do your parents have a problem

                      F
with you bringing food up to me

C   Em
Is it my new Hitler moustache?

        F   C
    Am I making enemies

                              Em
Telling your mom the house

             F   C
    looks like a shanty

                        Em
But it's still way classier than my

             F   G
    old meth lab in El Sobrante

(Chorus)

(Chorus)

F   C
How long, baby, til you turn 18?

F
Come on & drop out &

            C
    hang outside with me

A#
We can hang out at the bridge

        Dm
    & smoke a lot

A#   F
And maybe we can sell

                C
    the 8th graders pot (x2)

JORNADEROS

```
C            D          G              Em              C    D G Em
Why are all these Mexicans standing on the streets of San Rafael?
C            D               G               Em          C  D G Em
Doesn't it make you feel weird to see them eating food at Taco Bell?
C            D               G              Em
Crammed like clowns into the king cab of the Chevy
             C         D        G              Em
And the gringo contractor thinks they all speak Spanish
             C         D        G
But it's more complicated than that
C            D
Why are all these Mexicans
   G              Em               C    D G Em
   standing on the streets of San Rafael?
C            D          G
Was it some TV show that made them think
        Em                      C      D G Em
        that they should leave their home?
         C        D        G              Em
The corn is cheap; it's no way to make a living
         C        D             G              Em
All roads point north, with lots of hiding out and swimming
         C        D          G
So folks they'll never meet can make a killing
      Em         D            C                   D
Jornaderos, Jornaderos We're really sorry about the talking perros
      Em         D            C                   D
Jornaderos, Jornaderos If they pay you, will it be in Ameros?

C            D          G              Em              C    D G Em
Why are all these Mexicans standing on the streets of San Rafael?
C            D               G               Em          C  D G Em
Doesn't it make you feel weird to see them eating food at Taco Bell?
         C        D     G       Em
A border works just like a coffee filter
         C              D              G              Em
that you've filled too much now there's chunks in the espresso
             C         D        G              Em
And the mess you've made wouldn't fit in a sombrero
         C         D        G
That would give shade to every jornadero
```

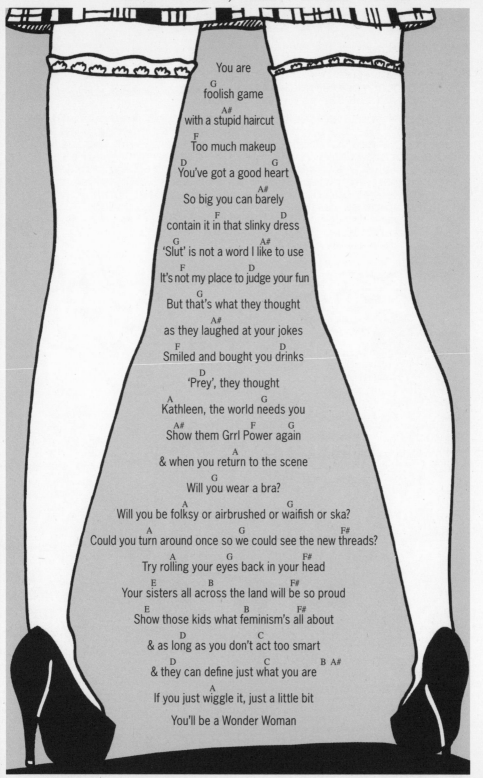

You are
G
foolish game
A#
with a stupid haircut
F
Too much makeup
D   G
You've got a good heart
A#
So big you can barely
F   D
contain it in that slinky dress
G   A#
'Slut' is not a word I like to use
F   D
It's not my place to judge your fun
G
But that's what they thought
A#
as they laughed at your jokes
F   D
Smiled and bought you drinks
D
'Prey', they thought
A   G
Kathleen, the world needs you
A#   F   G
Show them Grrl Power again
A
& when you return to the scene
G
Will you wear a bra?
A   G
Will you be folksy or airbrushed or waifish or ska?
A   G   F#
Could you turn around once so we could see the new threads?
A   G   F#
Try rolling your eyes back in your head
E   B   F#
Your sisters all across the land will be so proud
E   B   F#
Show those kids what feminism's all about
D   C
& as long as you don't act too smart
D   C   B A#
& they can define just what you are
A
If you just wiggle it, just a little bit

You'll be a Wonder Woman

ROCK 'N' ROLL TIPS

One key element of the rock'n'roll lifestyle is cheap rent. Yet in order to be truly free to live that same lifestyle at full volume, you must have permissive or nonexistent neighbors. Therefore, if a vacancy opens up near your home or practice space, it is your duty to keep that space vacant for as long as possible.

Get to know your local realtor; know their schedule and what their vehicle looks like. On days when they might be showing a vacant house in your neighborhood, have a house party with the loudest, most obnoxious bands you can find. If you see the realtor's car outside one of the vacant houses, it means they are showing the property to prospective tenants. Quick, gather everyone in the house and head to the practice space! Turn up the amps as loud as they will go. Turn to a random page in this book and begin practicing. This should keep the house vacant, and your rent at an acceptable level.

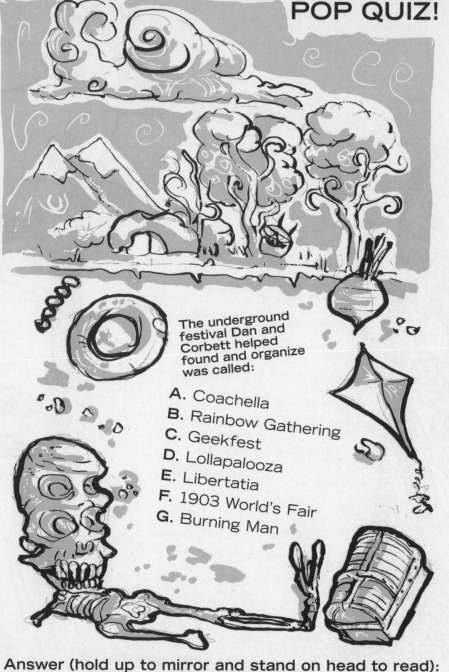

POP QUIZ!

The underground festival Dan and Corbett helped found and organize was called:

A. Coachella
B. Rainbow Gathering
C. Geekfest
D. Lollapalooza
E. Libertatia
F. 1903 World's Fair
G. Burning Man

Answer (hold up to mirror and stand on head to read):

Both C and E are correct. Libertatia grew out of a collaboration between Geekfest and the Pirate Punx.

After years of doing algebra & having wet dreams
_(F#m)_ _(G#)_

About the girls who gave it up
_(A)_

to the whole football team
_(E)_

It's time to go
_(F#m)_

So bring your yearbook and your favorite CDs
_(G#)_ _(A)_ _(E)_ _(F#m)_

& head upstate to work on some useless degree
_(G#)_ _(A)_ _(E)_ _(F#m)_

It's the best education Mommy can buy
_(B)_ _(C#)_

College! Now you're a full-fledged
_(F#)_ _(G#)_

productive member of society
_(A)_ _(E)_

Really, you're not just a tax writeoff for your family
_(F#)_ _(G#)_ _(A)_ _(E)_ _(F#m)_

Just don't knock over the bong
_(E)_ _(F#m)_

Or try to pierce yourself & get it wrong
_(E)_ _(Bm)_

Don't get it wrong
_(E)_ _(F#m)_

I love college, it's a great place to be
_(D)_ _(A)_ _(E)_ _(F#m)_

Nobody tells me what to do & I've got an identity
_(D)_ _(A)_ _(E)_

F#m   D
It feels so good; I'm on my own

      A
Mom & Dad don't know anything

   E
I don't tell them on the phone   A D

   A   D
I'm my own person

       A   D
I'm my own person

         F#m   E   F#m
& I can get piercings anywhere that I want

      F#m   E   F#m   A F#m A
I can get piercings anywhere that I want

F#m   G#
Four more years of drinking and dancing

     A   E   F#m
and boning the coeds down the hall

        G#
Four more years of avoiding

  A   E   F#m
any kind of work at all

      E   F#m   E
& if you run out of cash, don't distress

      F#m   E
Just send a polite request to

   F#m   E
your home address

   F#m   E   F#m   E   F#m
So you can buy more mushrooms

PUNK, YOU LET ME DOWN

Punk rockers talkin' talkin'
'Bout the way things used to be
They be talkin' 'bout how
   here and now
They 'bout to build the same old thing

They want a days-gone-by revival
To win that glory heyday gold
Just a tiny box of unoriginal thought
That be tastin' just like mold

Now I see that we must go
Must go our separate ways
But before we part I've got some more
Mean shit that I must say

You're like a newly filled up diaper
That's been thrown out into traffic
Incredibly white and full of shit
Just waiting to be hit

The Ramones would tell
   your ass to shut up
They wouldn't want you around
I think its time to tell you, suckas
Punk, you let me down

Now the best branch of humanity
Would have a more diverse community
What's with all the shit-talking?
And while I'm at it here's a few
   more things...

I wanted to be friends with you
But you got a real bad attitude
You're hiding so much; Who are you?
Why don't you tell the truth?

Peace out, sayonara, adios, au revoir
I can see that you are talkin'
All I hear is blah blah blah

It's good to know that someone
Can sing the awful truth
And I know for sure that someone
Sure as hell ain't you

I don't know what you've been sold
But punk rock is pushing 35 years old
And hey, I like some of those songs
But old people in spikes seems a little
   bit wrong

I got bored with 40s
   and the same three chords
But maybe I'm not who
   the form is for
Youth culture should really
   be left to the youth
Anarchism, catharsis,
   DIY, and the truth

Are just elements kids
   can make relevant again
Mixing, matching and
   adapting to environments
Fetishizing the 80s won't
   make a space safe
You think cassette tapes
   will mitigate date rape?

I hate this jaded-ass ritual nostalgia
Your shit gives me auditory
   fibromyalgia
If you're really smashing
   the state, great!
First break the chains
   and the spikes
   of the fashion state

The Ramones would tell
   your ass to shut up
They wouldn't want
   you around
I think its time to
   tell you, suckas
Punk, you let me down

REAL COOL

(Instrumental Intro) D A E A D A E A

A
What's your real name?

D
Where'd you come from?

E
You're trying too hard

A
and then some

A
Your strut is stuffy,

D
your slang ain't the best

E   D
Givin' the stinkeye,

A
you should give it a rest

D
We will be there

A
to make fun of your hair

E
Oh yes we will,

A
and that'll be real cool

D
And when the hair

A
is no longer there

E   A
We'll be there making fun

(Chorus)

And it's OK you came

from far away

To make bad music by

the Frisco Bay

But when you start

with that cold cold
shit

Like it's a game and

you're in it to win it

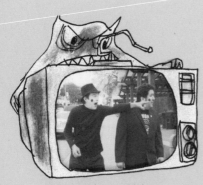

You grew up normal,

you're not that weird

Drinks in the City,

tight shirts and beards

Poor Rock'n'Roll is

crying in the rain

Cause its ranks are now filled

with a bunch of
fuckin' shit-stains

(Chorus)

SIDEBURNS

G   (F#)   Em   Em7 C
Give me a reason to believe to believe that
                            D
                you deserve another drink   G
G   (F#)   Em   Em7   C
You look like ass & you're consumed by boredom and
                        pretentiousness   D
G   (F#)   Em   Em7   C
The years will grind behind you, leaving you without a clue
                                              D
G   (F#)   Em   Em7   C
Just keep on working & on Fridays keep on playing pool

                                  (Chorus)

C   D   C
The toilet seat is so cool So refreshing to my face
        C   D   G Em   G
Everyone's got sideburns again Sideburns every place
      (F#)   D
            Sideburns every place
What do you do when you're too old to really have fun
     (F#)   Em   Em7   D
     but you want to look cool? Get off your ass
     Em7   C   G   (F#m)   Em
And set it down upon a swivelling bar stool
G   (F#)   Em   Em7
You're in that special age group when
          (F#)   D
          if you drink no one cares
     G   Em   Em7   C
But if you say you drink with certain people
                  D
     you might get somewhere
                  (Chorus)

28

D   A
Don't look in my eyes
D   G
Don't look in my eyes
D   A
Be afraid to look at me 'cause
G   D
I'm a scary guy
D   D   G
I paid the fare just like you
D   A
& you probably think you know
                        D
where I'm going to
C   G
The carpets are many colors
C
which all make brown
C   G
It's easy to clean up the mess left
A
by the guy downtown
A#   A
This train is bound for somewhere
C   G
I don't know because my
            D
eyes are down
D   A
Look at your newspaper

                              G
Look at your newspaper
D   A
The one you picked up off the floor
G   D
so you could comfortably stare
D   A   D G
I don't recall being told
D   A
When what you flush down
            D
became wet gold
C   G   C
The five-year-old didn't avert
            G
her gaze
C   G
She just kept chewing on
            A
her milky way
A#   A
This train is bound for somewhere;
C   G
I don't know because my
            D
eyes are down (x2)

29

VANILLA AMERICAN

Dm   A7
Picture perfect plastic people, custard cash cake and lies

A#
Stand with perfect posture

Gm   C
With your wide and empty eyes

Dm   A7
Blood is made of gasoline, heart attack at hardware store

A#
Now it's getting hard to breathe

Gm   C
Big cleanup on Aisle Four

(Chorus)

Gm   Dm
You must go around snatching brains

Gm   Dm
Cause I've heard this shit somewhere before

Gm   Dm
When you start to flap your ketchup-speckled trap

C   G   A
I hear Grandpa's drunken rants from '64

Gm   A
Cruel and out of breath

Gm   A
You're a darling citizen

A# C   A
That's you, Vanilla American

Dm   A7
Endangered species sausage, bread baked in a Nazi hearth

A#
Plate is carved from ancient oak

Gm   C
Drinking baby tears

Dm   A7
Christmastime and Halloween, Valentine's and Thanksgiving

A#   Gm   C
If religion's not your thing, blow it all at Burning Man

(Chorus)

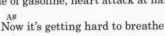

A
I'm hip I'm cool

C#
I'm on a first-name basis with the people

F#m
Who do the things I want to be

E
They'll take me out and buy me drinks

A
Girls will pay attention

C#
They will want to party with me

F#m
& buy me food, & they'll tell their friends

E
& that is how my legend begins

A
With my newfound status

C#
I'll try to get into places free

F#m
& bring some toadies too

E
Vicarious friends for vicarious fame

A
I hung out at the bridge

When I was in 9th grade

C#
& I gave my lunch to the hessians

F#m
So they wouldn't throw me in the creek

E
I liked that better than what I've got now

A
I'm hip I'm cool

C#
I'm on a first-name basis with the people

F#m
Who do the things I want to be

E
They'll take me out and buy me drinks

WE'RE SEVERE

I will try despite my nature,
[F]
'cause if I do the pros will snore
[A#]   [C]
Immersion in canned hurt I admit can be such a bore
[Dm]   [A#]   [C]
Please ignore its mention and ascension
[Dm]   [A#] [Dm]   [A#]
From what makes a really great band
[G] [F]   [C] [G]

(Chorus)

So I won't say I
[C]
Me won't tell the story about how me was feeling
[F]   [C]
So I won't say I
[C]
And then I'll be up on the all-time greatest ceiling
[F]   [C]
I'm down here and you're up there
[A#]   [F]
where they all have painted hair
[A#]   [F]
Bright and loud like Las Vegas
[G]
You're up there and we're down here
[A#]   [G]
Where nights consist of pot and beer
[A#]   [G]

32

A#
And you can't hear what we're calling you
                                    G
(Chorus)

        G
I'll try to come up staring
              G#
  with my fireworks exploding
              A#   C
  and my amps set at 11
G
And me and my manly howl
                        G#
  will climb the stairs to rocker heaven
A#   A#   C
I don't want that
A#   F
You can have that
A#   F
I have laughed back
          F

          G
(Spoken) Pardon the use of 'I' sir,
  I'll get back to work immediately
(Chorus)

33

The Bobby Joe Ebola

SONGBOOK #2

Children & Animals

DID YOU KNOW?

Corbett owns and cares for 30 birds of various species, several of whom rarely breed in captivity. He regularly contributes to the Humane Society, and also shares three cats and two dogs with his wife, Melissa. (So knock it off with the Burt Lancaster "Birdman Of Alcatraz" jokes.)

WRITERS ~ DAN ABBOTT & CORBETT REDFORD /// EDITOR ~ JASON CHANDLER
CONTRIBUTING ILLUSTRATORS (SEE APPENDIX FOR DETAILS): A. PHILLIPS,
C. ROAD, W. SMITH, J. CHANDLER, J. COTTERILL, P. AGUILERA, D. PAULOS,
P. SORFA, E. WHY, K. MCCARTHY, M. CLEM, D. MCFADZEAN, M. FOXALL, R. BUCHER

IT'S NOT WHAT YOU THINK!

People have often wondered why so many of our songs concern children and animals. Any performer worth their salt has probably heard the W.C. Fields quote. And it's true. Cute is the low-hanging fruit of entertainment. It sells, but somehow the saccharine cuteness of kids and critters poisons any greater point you might want to convey. It's like some crazy bleach on the logical brain. Still, animals and children keep showing up in our songwriting. Creepy, right? We should be writing about chicks and cocaine.

Is it our subconscious desire to have children, and Kronos-like fear of being a crappy parent that makes us sing about child-eating?

Do we loathe and resent the human race so much that we identify more with the animal kingdom? Perhaps our songs

are our children, and putting kids into songs is the closest we'll get to breeding. We certainly like being around both animals and children; they are unclouded by much of the bullshit that is responsible for the world's ills. Whatever problems society may have, it is not the fault of children or animals, and it is from the child or animal within us that we often take inspiration.

Perhaps the answer lies in our own childhoods; Corbett was the oldest of six, in a deeply dysfunctional household and was surrounded by pets. Dan was an only child until he was 10, and had more in common with his grandparents than his classmates. Neither of us have kids. As far as the animals, Dan grew up in a house full of eight large akitas, so his childhood was full of dogs stealing food from his plate and interacting with his much-younger sisters. "The Dog Ate The Baby," for example, was written while Dan, at 16, babysat his sisters. In adulthood Corbett has a menagerie of beloved dogs, cats and birds, and a plethora of cat-related tattoos. See, not that creepy after all, right? Right?

🐛 Bobby Joe Ebola Songbook #2 ~ TABLE OF CONTENTS

1 1/2 FT. (THE SQUIRREL SONG)

      D   A
When Bobby was 18 he met his Peggy Sue

     G   D   A
They'd hang outside the malt shop 'cause they had nothing else to do

    D   A
But then one starlit night ol' Bobby looked into her eyes

      G   A   D
& said "Baby, I really respect you tonight"

D
In the maternity ward

A
9 months down the road

      G   D   A
Bobby held Peggy's hand as she dispensed with her load

    D   A
The doctor said she gave birth to a squirrel

      G   A   D
& ol' Bobby's tail began to curl

(Chorus)

G   D
How do you help a lonely boy who don't know he's a squirrel?

A   D
Wandering over the grass in the business park

      G   D
& how do you convince a rodent that he has a big fuzzy tail

       C   G   D
& that his head is smaller than a tomato?

D   A
The press they had a field day in that tiny refinery town

           G   D   A   D
Peggy's parents kept her inside so that she would not be found

                                         A
Bobby snuck in through her window 16 days a week

        G   A   D
& stuffed his nuts into Peggy's cheeks

(Chorus)

D   A
Siberia is too cold for me if I don't wear no clothes

           G   D   A
When I sneeze everything freezes on the way out of my nose

D   A
So I'll wear a big fuzzy hat to show solidarity

           G   D   A
For the brave Siberians who don't have no fuzzy hats like me

(Chorus)

39

BIOLOGICAL IMPERATIVE

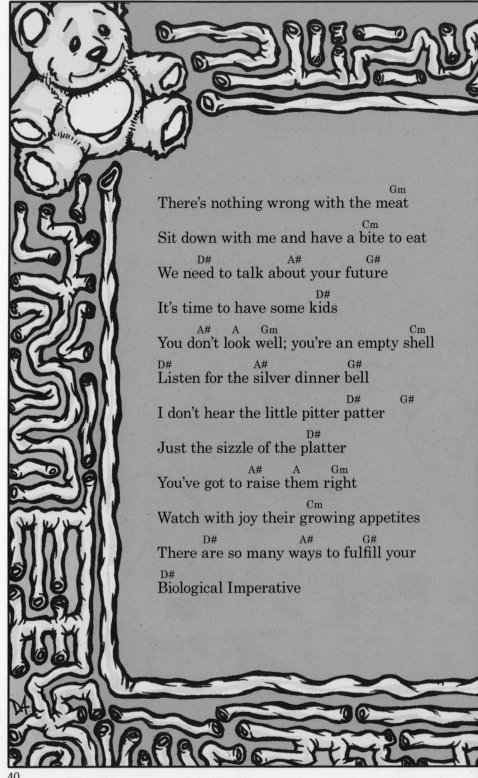

There's nothing wrong with the meat

Gm

Sit down with me and have a bite to eat

Cm

We need to talk about your future

D#   A#   G#

It's time to have some kids

D#

You don't look well; you're an empty shell

A#   A   Gm   Cm

Listen for the silver dinner bell

D#   A#   G#

I don't hear the little pitter patter

D#   G#

Just the sizzle of the platter

D#

You've got to raise them right

A#   A   Gm

Watch with joy their growing appetites

Cm

There are so many ways to fulfill your

D#   A#   G#

Biological Imperative

D#

     G#   D#
& the cellar's dark & cool

You don't want to spoil them

     G#   D#
They'll try to stay out late

But you can foil them

C#   G#
Chubby fingers through the bars of a cage

C#   G#
Grubby faces streaked with little tears

D#
Cowering cowering

                    Gm   Cm D# A# G#
From the flashlight beam

      Gm
Dinner time!

      Cm
Dinner time!

 D# A#   G#   Gm
Dinner Time!

BUNGEE BIRTH

G   D
Who had a baby in the bathroom?
G   A   B C B   A   F#
Who tried to convince us she was never pregnant?
G   D
Who tried to flush it down but almost died because

            Am   Em   D
She didn't know she had to cut the umbilical cord?
          D   C
Can you tell that kind of thing from the look in her eyes
      D   C   Em
A mixture of shock and pain and surprise

    A
Burst blood vessels in her eyes

    G   F#   F   E
Baby baby baby baby
    G   F#   F   E
Whoops baby whoops baby
    G   F#   F
Baby baby baby

G   D
I know a secret; I was listening at the door

G   D
I heard you flush 3 times, maybe it was 4

            Em   A
When you limped out you left a bloody trail
Em   A   Em
I saw you dragging your bloody purple tail
    G   F#   F   E   G   F#   F   E
Baby baby baby baby, Whoops baby whoops baby
    G   F#   F
Baby baby baby

CANARY

```
     D          G          D
There's a TV in every room except for mine
D        G              A        D
Fake flowers and trays of medicine
D          G                    D
Nobody ever leaves here unless they die
     G          G#         C#
Rusty wrinkled bodies and rotting minds
D            G             D
The old people babble incessantly
        D          G          D
With their endlessly monosyllabic refrains
D              G    A  D
The problems they have can be avoided
     G       G#          C#
But one larger problem still remains
```

(Chorus)

```
                      F#   Bm C#
You're outliving your teeth
                      F#   Bm C#
You're outliving your teeth
                 F#        Bm C#
Chewing mushy turkey
```

```
                      F#
You're outliving your teeth
          Bm          F#
You're outliving your teeth
          C#          F#
You're outliving your teeth

     D            G
I'm just here so the ones
                          D
   who still can see can see me
D                   G        A      D
I don't do a thing and maybe they identify
   with me
D
They too are locked up and
       G      A     D
   eat what they are fed
             G
Veins and sagging skin and
   G#                         C#
   brain activity clinging by a thread
```

(Chorus)

IT'S A SMALL WORLD

In 1996, Dan & Corbett saw Beat poet Allen Ginsberg perform in San Francisco. Ecstatic, they gave him a copy of their first CD. He grinned at the title and said, "Bobby Joe Ebola and the Children MacNuggits? Sounds like something Burroughs would be into."

Pinole and its unincorporated cousin El Sobrante have long been a breeding ground for noteworthy art and music. Metallica, Primus, and Creedence Clearwater Revival all have members who either went to school, grew up, or lived there at one time. The loose-knit assortment of weirdos at Pinole Valley High School in the late 80s (including members of Blatz, Isocracy, Green Day and others), formed an essential part of the 924 Gilman community that spawned the East Bay punk scene.

DOWN AT THE JAMBOREE

It was lost some time ago and
no one ever thought to look

For what was missing
was not written down in
some old dusty book

You could feel it more than see
it; like balance or like karma

Everything had its purpose and
we shared this place with honor

So I'm going to try to fix this break
between animal and man

I'm gonna start by tearin' apart
the way I make social plans

Won't throw some normal soiree
or give another boring party

It's time the world sees; fun
ain't just for you and me

Yes, next time I throw a shindig;
I'll be sure to save some seats

For those with whiskers, wings
and fins; four legs and furry feet

Now I'm not picky; don't protest
much; It's not like me to brag

But I'd rather head on down
to where it's all hops,
jumps and wags

Summon the fertile and the feral;
from the barnyard to the kennel

Open the coops and aviaries;
shoo the tops of the libraries

Invite the zoos and estuaries;
call the fleas and the bees

O'er the plastic in the seas; have
the beast and fowl and folk alike

Down at the jamboree

There's something special about
the kind of films I like to watch

Ones with kooky critters
cracking jokes and kicking
crackers in the crotch

I knew it as a little kid; I know
it more now that I'm older

Without our furry friends
around the world would
be a whole lot colder

So promise me next time you
have your friends over for food

That you set some places
at the table for your pets
and their friends too

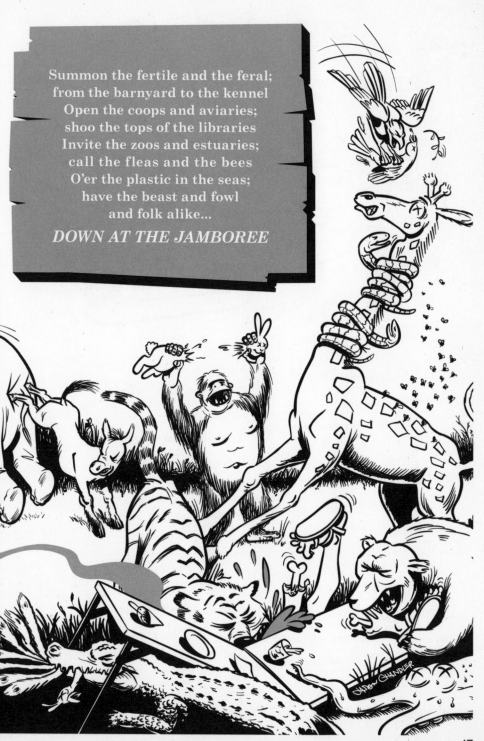

Summon the fertile and the feral;
from the barnyard to the kennel
Open the coops and aviaries;
shoo the tops of the libraries
Invite the zoos and estuaries;
call the fleas and the bees
O'er the plastic in the seas;
have the beast and fowl
and folk alike...

DOWN AT THE JAMBOREE

CHILD KILLER

E
    D   A   E
Help me off of this swing
    D   A   E
I am tired and nauseated
         D   A   F
I've been doing this since you told me to
   G   E
at gunpoint
        D   A   E
Broken lenses and a bloody nose won't
    D   A   E
stop me from getting home
       D   A
Crushed kneecaps, however
 F   G
Necessitate my hesitation

 D   A   G
'I need a taxicab', you might think I'd say
 D
But my tongue hangs out
      A   G
As you strangle me in the woodchips
 D   A   G
'I need a taxicab', you might think I'd say
 D
But my tongue hangs out
      A   G
As you strangle me in the woodchips

(Chorus)
G   A#
Childkiller, that's what you are
     Am   D7
Now the day looks brighter
G   A#
Childkiller, that's what you are
     Am   D7   G
Now there's one less human

               C   Am
Childkiller walks across the empty
         D7 A#E G
   parking lot
G   C   Am D7
Sweaty hands grip the chain-link fence
A#E G
          C   G   C   G
He can wait, but only for so long
                 C   D
'Cause they grow up oh so fast
And you've become

(Chorus)

E   A   E
The dog ate the baby while my family was away

E   A   E
Rover ate the baby; what will my mother say?

E
Well I don't care what they may say
A   D
I'm glad the baby's gone

E   D   C   E
And I say good good good, good dog

E   A
I came out of the bathroom and I heard
E
an awful sound

E   A
My little bro was wriggling,
E
tiny entrails on the ground

E
The dog ignored his high-pitched yelling
A   D
His soft head tasted like a melon

E   D   C   E7
Good good good, good dog

    A   E   D
My birthday was a-comin' Tuesday of next week

   A   E   D
Mom said it was OK to have a slumber party

    A   E   F#M   D
So I invited Dwayne, the kid with the ingrown brain

      A   F#M   E
And I invited John and his dad's collection of porno

    A   E   D
Bags of chips, soda, flashlights, dirty jokes

 A   E   D
Sleepy eyes & Thundercats, a pack of hidden smokes

 A   E   F#M   D
We were getting too loud, Dylan was the one who ripped one

 A   F#M   E
Mom knocked on the door & said 'Hey boys settle down'

 A   E   F#M   D
So she closed the door and I ran to the closet

       A   F#M   E
And pulled out Parker Brothers' mystifying oracle

(Chorus)

 A   E   D
I met Eazy through the Ouija

 A   E   D
I met Eazy through the Ouija

 A   E   D
I met Eazy through the Ouija

          F#M   E
And he said 'Awww yea!'

     A E D
Oh no!

                    A   E
He said 'Hey you sucka homies,
          D
      how the fuck you livin'?
   A   E   D
I hope you don't have any of the diseases
      I was given
   A   E   F#M   D
How is my dawg Ren? And what is up with
      Dre?
   A   F#M
And if you see that bitch-ass Ice Cube
   E
Tell him I said hey!'

(Chorus)

                      A   E
He said 'you're lucky they don't let you into
          D
      Heaven fully strapped
          A   E   D
'Cause if I had my AK, boy, I'd have to
      bust a cap
   A   E   F#M
Stay away from bad shit, I'm telling you
              D
you should
                   A   E
'Cause if not when you die you'll be
   F#M
A ghost rider in the hood'

(Chorus)

ROCK 'N' ROLL TIPS
How to put on a show

So, you've got a band. Unless you're holed up in a room somewhere sequencing fart noises, you'll eventually need to perform for people. Real people. In the same room. If you're lucky, maybe clapping.

If you're connected and attractive and have talent, you probably don't need this advice. Or this book, for that matter. But what if you're just starting out, or you're homely, awkward and weird? That was us, and we found it hard to book shows early on. We and our friends needed shows, though. So we created our own festival, an illegal outdoor series of concerts we called Geekfest. We made mistakes and wasted a ton of energy and money. But we learned a few things along the way, and these we pass on to you, so you can build your own Temporary Autonomous Zone.

LOCATION, LOCATION, LOCATION – Find a place nobody cares or knows about. Ideally this will be at the end of a long, unmarked dirt road far from any law enforcement or medical care. Look for pools of standing water. This means fun!

GET THE WORD OUT! – For illegal shows, find creative ways to let people know. Cops have computers too, so you must be subtle to deter them from attending. If you occasionally commit grisly crimes, for example, resist the temptation to leave flyers in the victims' hands. You could instead get a dedicated phone line and record incoherent, rambling directions on the outgoing message.

REFRESHMENTS – It doesn't matter how amazing you think your band is. As soon as the beer is gone, people are going to take off. Be OK with that, or get more beer. Also, if this is an overnight event, you should probably make a big pot of food. Cannibalism is not a made-up thing. It can happen to you and your friends.

CREW – There is a lot to do at a show. Get some friends to help. "Do it yourself" does not mean "do it alone." Music, like romance, is better with all your friends in the room heckling.

STAGE MANAGER – This person keeps the show running about an hour behind schedule, and may be the only one in the audience yelling "One more!"

SOUND GUY – This person keeps a running tally of how many microphones have been stolen, and makes sure every band has a tasteful amount of feedback.

SECURITY – This is the person who would ordinarily be kicked out of any other show for fighting. Place them at the entrance facing outward to keep violence off the premises.

DOOR – This person sits inside the entrance checking their phone and taking money from people. At the end of the night, they will be extremely hard to locate.

A FEW OTHER THINGS TO REMEMBER WHEN PUTTING ON A SHOW:

– Get other people excited! Encourage people to bring food or dress up. Pick an uplifting costume theme like "Me in 20 Years" or "The Person My Ex Would Rather Date."

– Have an escape plan, just in case the cops show up. Remember, "Dave" invited you.

– If there are bands who have driven a long way to play your show, make sure to get them some gas money. $2-$3 should be totally fine. You don't want them stuck on your couch forever.

When we started doing shows, we had no idea what we were doing, and neither will you. Get used to it. You'll make mistakes, lose money, have equipment failure, and play for three drunk dudes who don't care. But somewhere within the Venn diagram of scabies, hangover, and reporting for community service, lies a little thing called rock'n'roll.

POP QUIZ!

Which of the following is a Bobby Joe Ebola release?

1. A Sausage Named Clarence
2. Brown Tide
3. Two Cats Running
4. Led Zeppelin XIVI
5. Tantric Oboe Lullabies
6. Whale Songs for Natural Birth

Answer: 1996's "Two Cats Running" was the first ever MacNuggits release. "A Sausage Named Clarence" is a rock opera the MacNuggits have performed during special occasions and intend to one day record. It has yet to be officially released.

IN THE BARREL SLIDE

```
D              G    A
We used to be together

D              G    A
We talked about the weather

D                G      A      D   G A
You were on the other side of a tetherpole

D            G      A
We never talked about it

D          G         A
You wouldn't acknowledge it

D                    G      A      D   G    A
I would have lowered their opinion of you
```

(Chorus)

```
     G                C                Am       D
But in the barrel slide and in the library aisle

         Em
You were different

       G            C          Am   D
And during quiet time you were so silent

       Em
And distant

D              G    A
A puddle by a fountain

D              G    A
Sand in the drain is drowning

D
You said you'd never
        G    A      D   G  A
  been in a heated pool

D              G      A
I said I hadn't either

D              G      A
Everyone saw me meet her

D                  G
You were the laughingstock
    A      D  G  A
of the entire school
```

(Chorus)

       C   D   Em
And I wondered why you never used a spoon

       C   D   Em
And I wondered why they never let me walk you home

       C   D   Em
And I wondered why you never used a spoon

       C   D   Em
And I wondered why they never let you see the sun

         C   D
Is there something you want to tell me

  C
Something you want to show me
                            D

  C   D   Em
What's that thing, & why's it glowing?

D   G   A
They moved in to get her

D   G   A
She did them one better

D   G   A   D   G A
Proving her loyalty to them once and for all

D   G   A
I didn't see it coming

D   G   A D
I would have started running

                           G
Her purple tentacle impaled me

     A   D   A   G
  against a wall

(Chorus)

55

HERMIE HALBERT

<pre>
     C   Am   F   G
Swimming round his mayo jar, minding his own biz
     C   Am   G
Lived little Hermie Halbert, the abrasive Tourette's fish
     C   Am   F   G
Hermie was a harsh one, his words they cut like knives
     C   Am   F   G
Hermie was a foulmouthed sailor in a former life
</pre>

(Chorus)

<pre>
     C   Am
Hermie'd scream "Fuck," and Hermie'd scream "shit!"
     F   G   C Am F G
And twitch and unwind from his fit
</pre>

<pre>
C   Am
Hermie was bought by a kid named Joe
F   G
All was going swell

     C   Am
Joe took his fish to Sunday school
     F   G
The teacher brought up Hell
          C   Am
He said 'Satan lives beneath us
F   G
In a fiery place'
          C   Am
'When you lie and cheat and rape and steal
     F   G
It's him you'll have to face'
</pre>

(Chorus)

<pre>
C   Am   F   G
Hermie was incarcerated in a block of lead
     C   Am   F
They left him in a building foundation
     G   C
Left him for dead
     Am
100 years later
     F   G
When they tore the building down
     C   Am
A lowly non-union construction worker
     F   G
heard an awful sound
</pre>

(Chorus)

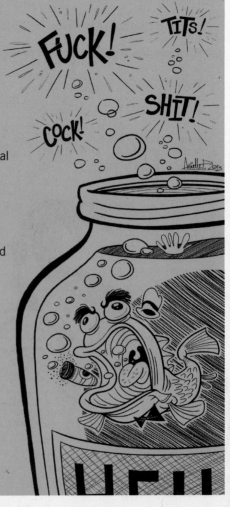

56

It is time, peck the lock, free the
    whole cell block
Everybody knows what's up, we are
    birds in one big flock
Call it off, ring the bell
This is a strange little sliver of hell
It's no fun & it smells like hay and
    oyster shells

Hey hey hey everybody!
What happened to your smiles?
For that big bad wheel to lose its tread
It's going to take a few more miles
Hey hey hey everybody! Hey hey hey
    everybody!
Don't be afraid to get your feathers
    dirty

Do you feel it in your wings?
It's so cold it stings
It is freezing like the snow,
    but now we're going home
They are shit out of luck
Frankly they are fucked
& they'll wish that they were never
    born when these robins come to rock

Hey hey hey everybody! Build your nest in rusty gears
They can't kill two with a single stone if the sky is never clear
Hey hey hey everybody! Hey hey hey everybody!
The crumbs they threw us taste a little bloody

TASHIROJIMA (THE STORY OF CAT ISLAND)

$\qquad$ Dm $\qquad$ C
There is an island; Tashirojima

F
It is in Nippon

Dm
It is small

$\quad$ C
In the Pacific

F
And no dogs are let on

$\quad$ G $\qquad$ F
Every person on this island

$\quad$ C $\quad$ Dm
Is very very old

$\quad$ G $\qquad$ F
And the cats outnumber people there

$\quad$ C $\qquad$ Dm
Or so I have been told

$\qquad$ C $\qquad$ F
The people of Cat Island go fishing to
$\quad$ survive

$\qquad$ Dm
They respect the cats

$\qquad$ C
Feed them scraps

And the cats eat all the mice

$\quad$ G $\qquad$ F $\qquad$ C
In America, there are no "neko jinga"

$\qquad$ Dm
anywhere in sight

$\quad$ G $\qquad$ F $\quad$ C
If we put these cat shrines up cats
$\quad$ might

$\qquad$ Dm
steer us right

$\qquad$ F $\qquad$ C $\qquad$ Dm
Like they did on the island that night

$\quad$ Dm $\qquad$ C
A large earthquake woke the cats

F
From the belly of the deep

$\quad$ Dm $\qquad$ C
Only they could hear its rumble

$\qquad$ F
Most humans still asleep

$\quad$ G $\qquad$ F
So the cats began to march

$\quad$ C $\qquad$ Dm
To the island's highest peak

$\quad$ G $\qquad$ F
The sight of kittens on parade

C   Dm
Made the people think

   Dm   C
Why do the cats flee the coast?

   F
Away from fish and bait

Dm   C
If we do not follow them

F
What will be our fate?

        G   F   C   Dm
In America, there are no "neko jinga" anywhere in sight

        G   F C   Dm
If we put these cat shrines up cats might steer us right

           F   C   Dm
Like they did on the island that night

LIFE OF PET

A   D
I wish I could shit on anything and not
   get thrown in jail

A   C#
Claw up all the nice things & bask in
   the sun all day

D   A
I want to lick my privates in front of

      F#
  everyone

G   D A   A D
Live the life of pet, live the life of fun

(Chorus)

             A D
Lick the butter

            A D
Fuck my brother

               A D
Eating lots of spiders

               A D
Sleeping when I'm tired

     A   D
But alas I have to work many hours a day

    A   C#
I never have a second for frolic or for play

    D
But sometimes when I'm all alone and

A   F#
No one is around

   G   D
I get down on all fours

   A   A D
And make a kitty sound

(Chorus)

   A   D   A   D
Cat Man Cat Man Cat Man Do

A   D   A   D
Running all around burying poo

   A   D
Jump spring pounce shake

   A   D
Shake some more

A   D   A   D
Slide slide slide on the kitchen floor

E   F#m11#5   E
How nice that you aren't now

            F#m11#5   D
Good of you to be a cow

          A
Alone along a line of little leaves

E   F#m11#5   E
Fluffy children floating in the breeze

     E F#m11#5
    F#m11#5   E
Tiptoe through her lips and slip

    F#m11#5   D
Upon a peel beneath the trees

       A
Arrange a greater fantasy to find

E   F#m11#5   E   F#m11#5
Silent children hanging from their minds

(Chorus)

C   G
Call me cold and grey

A#
Here's what you will say

F   C   G
To keep me smiling and alive in the hay

   E F#m11#5 E F#m11#5
E   F#m11#5
Mr. Turtle wake up and scream

    E   F#m11#5 D
You're being evicted in a shallow stream

    A
Here I come to smash your little home

   E F#m11#5 E F#m11#5
Into a stone

E   F#m11#5
Poor Mr. Turtle has no home

E
Wanders through the hemlock

F#m11#5   D
All alone
What can he do!

   A
With body blue and broken spine

    F#m11#5   E
Legs drag limp along the ground

   F#m11#5
behind

(Chorus)

SPENDING CHRISTMAS ON CRACK

G   D
Rudolph the rabid rottweiler had a very foamy mouth

                                     G
And if you ever saw him, he would start to bark and growl

                                    D
All of his white trash masters used to tie him to a chain

                                 G
They never pet poor Rudolph, 'cause he had a case of mange

C   G   C   G
Then one foggy ghetto night the police came to say

D
Rudolph with your chain so tight, don't get loose, you'll surely bite'

G   D
Then the pig bastards shot him, 'cause the neighbor made a plea:

                               G   Em F G
Kill off that stupid mongrel, he's a carrier of rabies

G   Em   F   G
I asked my mother, 'Do you believe in Santa Claus?' one Christmas eve

G   Em
She took a hit from her enormous crack pipe

               F   G
And she said 'Son, son I believe'

G   Em
She said, 'When Christmas Eve comes,

       F   G
    better get yourself hidden well out of sight'

       G   Em   F   G
'Cause son, don't you understand, his suit used to be white'

(Chorus)

G   Em   F   G
Santa Claus is a cannibal, his suit is stained red

G   Em   F   C   G   F
Santa Claus kills anyone who sees him so get your ass to bed

          C   G
Get your ass to bed

G   Em   F   G
One hundred years ago in a tiny village outside of Berlin

G   Em
There lived a kind man, a beloved toymaker

F   G
Until he began to eat his kin

G   Em   F   G
The villagers rose up in rage but when they reached his home

G   Em
They found a sleigh, all a-filled with toys

       F   G
Completely made of bones

(Chorus)

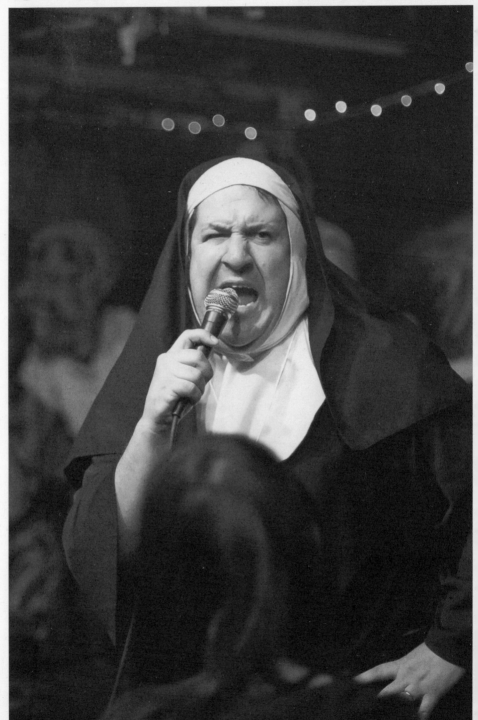

The Bobby Joe Ebola
SONGBOOK #3

Love & Other Mistakes

DID YOU KNOW?

Corbett's grandparents, the Scolaris, are upstanding citizens who have played a major role in Pinole's development. The Scolaris were voted Man & Woman of the Year multiple times, and have been honored with their names on various bronze plaques around the city. They once owned the Pinole landmark, The Pythian Castle, and Corbett's grandmother ran the kissing booth at the annual fair for many years. They don't quite know what to make of Corbett.

Love & Other Mistakes

WRITERS ~ DAN ABBOTT & CORBETT REDFORD /// EDITOR ~ JASON CHANDLER
CONTRIBUTING ILLUSTRATORS (SEE APPENDIX FOR DETAILS): P. SORFA,
J. CHANDLER, W. SMITH, T. CELEMIN, C. MOORE, A. PHILLIPS, B. PINKEL,
M. A. TURNER, P. AGUILERA, R.Z. RIFFEY, K. MCCARTHY, B. CATMULL,
B. ZABLACKIS, M. CLOTFELTER

PLEASE DON'T GET ANY ON ME

Rock'n'roll is a funny animal, so deeply intertwined with the teenage American libido. The word itself comes from slang for having sex in a car. So it is no surprise that a great majority of songs in rock are about love and sex. We at Bobby Joe Ebola have certainly had our ups and downs with romance. Dan spilt barrels of ink over unrequited teenage love, and Corbett has fallen head over heels in love more times than he can count. The band owes its existence to one of those crushes; our first show was a terribly awkward bit of mating plumage.

But our artistic inclinations tend to lead us in different directions. That's a danger-

ous trait for a band. If you write songs that aren't about sex, drugs and rock'n'roll (rock'n'roll, like a teen-

ager, is not only lustful but narcissistic), you risk being tarred with adjectives like "quirky" or "novelty." Then hardly anybody will have sex with you, and in that case,

why be in a band at all?

We just can't help ourselves though. Anyway, there are plenty of love songs already, probably better than we could write. Let other bands serenade you from the garden. We will dig up the worms and fling them at your balcony. Love is a messy, general term for a variety of experiences. The songs in this collection are some of our attempts to look at the underside of love; its dead ends and abandoned corridors. A word of warning, however: you may enjoy playing these songs, but DO NOT attempt to seduce anyone with them. You will crash and burn. Don't say we didn't warn you!

🌿 Bobby Joe Ebola Songbook #3 ~ TABLE OF CONTENTS

ANNE

GCG   G   C   G C
I'm in love with your mom, so don't get pissed.

       Em   F   G C
'Cause this is LOVE, not just sex.

      G   C   G C
It's despite the point that she gives good head.

          Em   F   G
I'm more into her eyes and her mind instead.

    Em
We could live in a house on a hill

     D
with a dog and a stereo.

    B
You'd get your own room.

(Em)

I DON'T WANT TO BE YOUR DAD I JUST WANT TO BE YOUR (D) BRO

B
Maybe you could bear the ring.

Em
But there's some things about your mom

D
that you wouldn't want to know.

B   G C G
and so you'll hear me sing.

C
I'm in love with your mom, so don't get pissed.

Em F   G C
'Cause this is love, not just sex.

G   C
It's despite the point that she gives good head.

Em F   G
I'm more into her eyes and her mind instead

THE CRAZY

```
G        Am           C           D    G
I don't want to go outside today
            Am              C            D              G
Things are getting just a little too weird even for me
        Am            C        D G         C              D              G
But if you can make it over here,   we can toast the end of everything
              Am         C       D G
It doesn't matter who started it
              Am          C           D             G
A brand new flag is waving on every stinking station
          Am            C        D G         C              D
Maybe when you've had a little sleep,    you'll be better conversation
G              C    G              C
Do you need a car? Do you need a house?
G                 Em              C    D
Do you need some shelter from the radiation?
G              Am             C             D
You can crash on my couch and wait for the light to fade
        G              C         D    G
And I'll shoot you at the first sign of infection
G       Am            C      D G    C              D
I'm not what you'd call sentimental & it was always complicated
      G        Am          C         D G    C              D
Even if we remain things will never be the same, and we're already changing
      G              C       G              C
I build my house of steel, I build my house of lead
      G           Em            C    D
I seal myself in tight against the radiation
G           Am            C         D  G    C              D
You seem all right but I am keeping on the light just in case you try to kill me
  G            C      G              C      G              Em
I let you in my house, I guess that I was wrong, maybe these things aren't
  C    D
 contagious
```

G   Am   C   D
Bandage up that scratch, I've got a pitchfork and a bat

G   C   D
Maybe Seal was right about the Crazy

G   C   G   C
Do you need some cards? Do you need some dice?

G   Em   C   D
Killing time and waiting for the radiation

               G   Am   D   G
I've got Sorry, I've got RISK, the Game of Life is missing pieces

                   C
Why don't you check down in the basement?

G   C   G   C
Do you need a car? Do you need a house?

G   Em   C   D
Do you need some shelter from the radiation

G   Am   C   D
You can crash on my couch and wait for the light to fade

               G   C   D   G
And I'll shoot you at the first sign of infection

FREAKY BABY

           G   A#
You got that Chelsea cut, you got no time for a scene

           G   A#
You got an interesting smell, I don't know where you been

        G   A#
You dive in the dumpster and as I walk past

             G   A#
You poke your head out and say, "Spare change for trash?"

(Chorus)

          G   A#
You a freaky baby, a straight sideways freak

        G   A#
The way you move is making me weak

          G   A#
You got drunk and cut your hair, them people stare

        G   A#
When it comes to freaks them others can't compare

          G   A#
Cos you a freaky baby (freaky)

  C   D#   G   A#
freaky baby (freaky) freaky baby (freaky)

G
Baby

      G   A#
You making me sweaty with all that gender bending

      G   A#
You squattin' that flat, C'mon and jiggle that

        G   A#
You make them vegans scramble, that booty's hard to handle

      G   A#
I want to make believe I'm your bicycle seat

  G   A#
Pass that 40 round and round

G   A#
Who needs chairs when you got the ground

    G   A#
Hold out your sign, take a rolly hit

     G
Tell them cops, "Eat shit!"

  A#
  Now chill for a bit

(add in your own rap
 breakdown here)

(Chorus)

IT'S A SMALL WORLD

For the Bobby Joe Ebola tracks on the Advice For Young Lovers 7" split with Your Mother, the band snuck into the Oakland practice space of metal band Testament and recorded through their enormous amps.

PINOLE FACTS

Pinole was originally inhabited by an Ohlone people called the Huchiun.

When Spanish soldiers got lost exploring the area around the San Francisco Mission, they ran out of food in an area overflowing with game, shellfish and edible greens.

They were rescued by the Huchiun, who rolled their eyes and fed them pinolli, a porridge made from acorn mush.

The grateful soldiers named the area Pinole, and as a show of thanks later enslaved the Huchiun and several other tribes.

I NEED POON

Am
Don't tell me I don't need this

Am
Don't abandon me with a kiss

  G   Dm
I love you and we'll be there soon

       Am
I need poon

Am
Tell me what will make you hot

Am
Give me everything you've got

G   Dm
Dress me up and stuff my ass with cookies

        Am
I need nookie

Am
I don't understand why you don't want to

Am   Dm
I just want to be a part of you, a part of you

      Am
Let's screw

C   G   C   G
I can't explain this aching in my balls

   C   G   D
or how you look to me when Mr. Willy calls

       C   G
And when I'm screaming alone

C   G
Late at night

      C   G   D
The stars are sticky and milky white

Am
Don't tell me that this will pass

Am
I want to nibble on your ass

   G   Dm
& pose for porno stardom til it hurts

       Am
I need to spurt

Am
It's OK if you want to stop

Am
I wish you hadn't called the cops

   G   Dm
When they walk in I'll jism across the room

      Am
They need poon

76

G#   A#
I don't miss your touch, never mind
  your kiss

    G#
Your eyes, your voice, your shaven

    A#
  head, none of that I miss

    G#   A#
You ask me why I love you, well I'll
  just tell you flat

      G#
It's the way you shit in my mouth,

    A#
  so baby please come back

(Chorus)

      G#   C#
'Cause you're the only one who

      D#
  understands me

    G#   C
So stand above me, my

      D#
  one and only

  G#
Some might call us sick, say what

      C#   D#
  we're doing isn't right

    G#   C#
But until you've tasted her shit you

      D#
  Shouldn't knock it 'till you've tried it

G#   A#
Straight from the tap, that's how
  I like my crap

G#
You've been holding back

    A#
  long enough

    G#   A#
So baby let it go, oh, oh, let your
  loving flow

  G#
I want a heaping helping of your

    A#
  loaf

(Chorus)

LIVER LOVER

```
A                      C      E
You may say it's strange but it is true
A                   C         E
I've finally found a way to replace you
A                 Am                    E
You were so frigid but our love still wouldn't keep
Am                  F                E
My new companion is inanimate and cheap
A                C    E
On the day she left me, I found
A                     C          E
My lover, my liver weighed only half a pound
A                Am                 E
A ziplock bag, a microwave and in went dinner
A              F        E
I made love to a dead cow's innards
```

(Chorus)

```
            A     C  G           D#   A# C#
'Cause I'm a Liver Lover, don't want no other
C#              G#        C G A
Gimme that soggy dead delight
      C  G            D#   A#
Lover! Liver! Just one warm sliver
    C#          G#        B
I won't need any onions tonight
```

LIVER

```
          A                                        C                        E
The space between the couch cushions is just right for me
A                                        C                  E
I'll slouch down with my baggy and do the nasty on my knees
A              Am                E
Everyone calls me the Liver King
A                             F                        E
But I'm so happy because it feels just like the real thing
```
(Chorus)
```
A                                    C                E
My roommates think I'm sick but I think it's great
A                              C              E
When I go shopping I almost always find a date
A                        Am              E
Liver won't treat me wrong, will never be untrue
A                           F                    E
And if I had a real girl I'd probably love her liver too
```
(Chorus)

MR. ABUSE

G   D   C
I'll pick you up at 7, not a second late

G   D   C
Take you to the movies, the same old
    blueprint date

G   D   C
Take you somewhere private, maybe to the Bay

G   Am   D
Park the car and hope to hear you say:

C   G
'Fuck me! Fuck me! Fuck me! Inside of me right now

    Em   B7
C'mon you big dumb jock boy, take me to the clouds

    C   G
Tear off your No Fear hat & your Mossimo shirt

    Em   B7
Tear off my velvet bra, I want to feel it hurt'

(Chorus)

      C
'Cause if you really loved me

     G
You'd put out tonight

D
Put out tonight

G   G7
Turn out the lights

C   G
Don't want to cling to a sinking ship

     D
Relationship

     G   G7
Don't want that shit

C
If you really loved me

     G
You'd pay for my beer

D   G
Is that a tear in your eye?

(Repeat Chorus)

81

ROCK 'N' ROLL TIPS

Booking a tour

Going on tour is an essential, and arguably the best, part of being in a band. After your fledgling band plays every club in your hometown, and everyone's heard the hastily-produced demo, home becomes a stagnant fishbowl. The applause becomes halfhearted and the performances become automated and predictable. It's the same people playing the same songs for the same people. And a known quantity does not make for an exciting Friday night.

For a band that is just starting out, the first tour takes on almost Homeric significance. Especially if the band is populated by fairly sheltered suburbanites whose knowledge of touring comes from wistful hair-metal ballads on MTV. This was more or less our mindset in 1996 when we resolved to hit the road on a brief jaunt. Which may help explain why the first place we went was L.A.'s Opium Den, ground zero for shattered dreams everywhere.

You, however, don't have to make the same mistake. You have a whole range of different mistakes to make. You have no booking agent, very little money, and a vehicle that would be worth more as a cube of glass and steel. You're ready to go on tour! So here are a few tips for booking your own tour:

1. START SMALL. Touring is not for everyone. Try a weekend jaunt of shows close to home. Treat it as a trial run before you and your bandmates take the time off work.

2. FINDING A VENUE OR BOOKER can be hit or miss the first time you venture into a city. Don't be shy about asking other bands where they've played. Also, the Internet can be your friend. If you're totally lost, search for "live music venues" in the city you're looking for, and look at the tour schedules of bands you like.

3. WRITE A BAND BIO. Nothing too fancy, just a description of what the band is about, and links to any online presence. You can paste this onto an email when you first approach a venue or booker.

4. THE U.S. IS VERY LARGE. We try to avoid driving more than 200 miles in a day. Some drives are unavoidable (I'm looking at you, Las Cruces to San Antonio), but long drives can be stressful and expensive. Google Maps is an excellent resource for planning this out. Also, do a little math and figure out how much you're going to need each day in food and gas. Do the math wrong and you will be eating each other at a rest stop in Wyoming.

5. WHERE DO YOU WANT TO BE on the weekends of your tour? If you don't have a draw, sometimes small to medium-size towns can be better weekend dates. There's less going on than in big cities, so it's more likely that local folks will come out to see an unknown band.

8. WHERE WILL YOU STAY while you're in town? Don't be shy about asking the booker if they can help in that area. People are generally hospitable wherever you go, and you may find yourself up all night sharing records, drinking beer and making lifelong friends. Or you may find yourself in some terrifying drunken nightmare with cops, broken glass and barking dogs. If you have a long drive the next day, make sure whoever is driving gets the bed, or the best sleeping spot.

9. IF YOU'RE PASSING NEAR A NATIONAL BORDER, make sure you're not "riding dirty." If you have drugs or dead bodies in the car, use them or lose them.

Yes, tour is exhausting, demoralizing, dangerous and unprofitable. Sounds fun, right? Hopefully these tips will help get you on the road, or will give you enough reasons to stay home.

POP QUIZ!

Connect Dan and Corbett with jobs they've held!

1. Barney the Dinosaur
2. doggy day care attendant
3. license plate frame vendor
4. Walmart drone (graveyard shift)
5. fast food drive through cashier (night shift)
6. substitute teacher
7. pizza delivery driver
8. telemarketer
9. janitor at punk club
10. security guard (one night)
11. seasonal apple picker
12. towel boy
13. dog shit cleanup

THE NEARLY OUT-OF-SALT CABARET

```
     F      A#      D#          C
But I can't see the mess they've made
  F       A#       D#     C
Can't point out the harm
      F          A#       D#     C
Can't feel that punch to my face
 F    A#     D#    C
Or my flaming arm
```

(Chorus)
```
      A#        C          F
Who cares about my broken fingers
A#     C     F
Or my missing cash
         A#      C
When I'm daydreaming
          F       A#
When I'm staring blankly
            C        F        A#
When I'm speaking, when I'm sleeping
           C        F
I'm stuck on the Galbreth girl
        A#                       F
She's at the controls She's at the controls
            C#    C
She's at the controls
                  F
We're gonna crash land
```

```
        F       A#      D#    C
So they're trying to pull me over
      F        A#        D#    C
Can't hear them when they talk
      F       A#      D#    C
The worst thing for me now
        F     A#    D#    C
Would be going for a walk
```

(Chorus)

POLY

G D C D D C   D G

     Bm   Am   D   G
We need a system, because I'm getting confused

     Bm Am   D   Am
A new dictionary for words I thought I knew

                      D   Am
Colored socks for hanging on the door

                         D
maybe you two could scoot on to the floor

        C   D
& I'll wear earplugs & gouge out my own eyes

(Chorus)

     G   D   C   G
She's poly-poly-poly-polyamorous It's glamorous and scandalous

     G   D   C   D
She's poly-poly-poly-polyamorous What's a man to do?

     G   D   C   G
She's poly-poly-poly-polyamorous The room smells like animals

   G   D   C   D   G
I'll carry this candle for you into the other room

     Bm   Am   D   G
We're both enlightened; You're not my property

     Bm   Am   D   Am
It's not a question merely of privacy

                               D
But now my old friends have come sniffing around

Am   D
Telling me they heard, and asking if you're around

     C   D
I just tell them take a number, like I do

(Chorus)

     G   D   C   G
She's poly-poly-poly-polyamorous I thought that I could handle it

     G   D   C   D
She's poly-poly-poly-polyamorous She's doing it all wrong

     G   D   C   G
She's really more like polysexual or omni-directional

     G   D   C   D   Em
There's got to be an ethical explanation why you're gone so long

Em   Bm   Am   D
I feel like my heart is handicapped or differently abled or whatever

     Em   Bm   Am   D
But I don't really know what you mean when you say the word together

G   Bm Am   D   G
Who is this person lying next to me

                Bm   Am   D
Who filled my squirtgun with liquid ecstasy?

Am   D
What if someone came home and got really depressed,

    Am   D
Attempted squirtgun suicide just for pretend

          C   D
Then they had to get up and go to the DMV?

(Chorus 2x; modulate the 2nd one up to begin on G#)

SHE AIN'T NO CRIP

G   C   E   D
How many times must I ask and from you get no reply?

G   C   E   D
About the cuts above your eyebrow or the bullet wound on your thigh

G   C   E   D
I found a loaded Beretta inside your dresser drawer

G   C   D
And I found a red bandana lying on the bedroom floor

(Chorus)

C   D   Em
My baby is a Blood, she's straight out of the hood

C   D   Em
My girl she ain't no Crip, I taste malt liquor on her lips

C   D   G   Em
She's rolling deep & causing crime, and my heart is doing time

C   D   C   G
My baby is a Blood and I'm scared

G   C   E   D
In your car I found an empty 40 and a 20-sack

G   C   E   D
And I heard your girlfriend whisper 'Yo Puta I got your back'

G   C   E   D
What happened to my little girl, the one I thought I knew

G   C   D
And how come when you buy your clothes they are no longer blue

(Chorus)

Em   C
She used to call me honey, & now she calls me 'G'

Em   C
We used to have a special thing, now it's a special thang

Em   C
She used to hold me closely & now she holds me up
(Chorus)

G   C   E   D
We got married and settled down like we'd dreamed of oh so often

G   C   E   D
We got a cozy little love nest in the deepest part of Compton

G   C   E   D
We had a get together to christen our new home

G   C   D
All of her friends taught all of my friends how to play Domino

(Chorus)

WRYTING LOVE SONGS (WILL NEVER HELP ME GET THE CHYCKS)

D   A   G   D
Writing love songs will never help me get the chicks
              A   G   A   D
Writing love songs will never help me get the chicks
   D   Bm
I gave you the key to my heart & you broke it off in the lock
   G   Em   A
I gave you the shoe to my soul, and you wore it around with no socks

(Chorus)
   D   Bm
Baby, can't you see
           Em   A   D
I'm lost without you and I'm making bad analogies
   D   Bm
I gave you the crackers of my confidence and you crumbled them all in my bed
   G   Em
I lent you the hat of my loneliness,
       A
Now there's bugs laying eggs in my head
   D   Bm
Baby, can't you see

              G   Em   A

I'm lost without you and I'm making bad analogies

D   A   G   A

Writing love songs will never help me get the chicks.

             A   G   A D

Only money and a big tattoo of 666.

      D   Bm

Now there's only so many times that my poor heart could be turned away

G   Em   A   D

But baby now I'm not even interested, 'cause now I am totally gay

(Chorus)

            D   Bm Em

Baby, you made me gay.

             A

Are you happy girl, I'm gay

            G   Em   A

But I'm not, so meet me backstage

YOU DEPRIVATION CHAMBER

```
      E                 A               E
They say that they can get my heart to call it quits
      E               A        E
That just two days and I'll get over it
      A                       B       A              B
All my friends chipped in for the bill but I can't wait until
      A             B        E       B
I get out of this place so I can call her
```

(Chorus)

```
            E                 B
I'm in a you deprivation chamber,
          A                     C     A
and I'm bangin against the walls
       E             B                A            C    A
Took away my pen and paper,  They won't let me make no calls
      E         B          C        A  B
I'm crying, I'm pouting, I'm whining
      E         B            C#      F#         B
I'm kicking, I'm screaming, I'm dying, Whah Whah Whah
```

```
      E              A           E
They say that I'm sexually repressed
             E                              A                E
When they show me all those inkblot things and I always see your breasts
```

```
          E                   A            E
The first thing they did was take away your picture
E                  A              E
Next they brought in a pile of Barely Legals
      A                  B       A                    B
Anything that they could do to make my life stop revolving around you
A                   B              E      B
All those suits know nothing about my will
```

(Chorus)

```
          E              A          E
They say that I am in the early stages
           E                    A              E
That my symptoms are drawn out into three phases
          E               A          E
They say the first is denial, but I don't think so
      A                   B                A                    B
They'll try to get my mind off you, feed me the words she said aren't true
      A             B        E      B
Those bastards say it's for my own good
```

(Chorus)

DID YOU KNOW?

Corbett spent his first few years living on a fruitarian commune near North San Juan, CA, where his mind was irreparably damaged by exposure to too much Canned Heat.

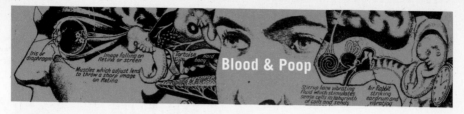

Blood & Poop

WRITERS ~ DAN ABBOTT & CORBETT REDFORD /// EDITOR ~ JASON CHANDLER
CONTRIBUTING ILLUSTRATORS (SEE APPENDIX FOR DETAILS): A. PHILLIPS,
P. SORFA, W. SMITH, R.Z. RIFFEY, J. CHANDLER, M. FOXALL, J. COTTERILL, S.
DIVELBISS, R. BUCHER, J. NOVAK, E. WHY, C. FORSLEY, K. STEIN, M. O'DRISCOLL

A STEAMING PLATE OF ARTISTIC FULFILLMENT

Life is gross. The biological nitty-gritty of existence is a little nauseating. Why is that, though? Is it the deeply-ingrained Judeo-Christian loathing of the physical that makes us look upon life with such disdain? Is it simply a terrified reaction to our temporal nature, the recognition that ultimately, we are merely meat and juices? The body is not intrinsically disgusting though; the meanings we attach to it are; the ideas and the connotations surrounding human functions that gross us out. Poop can simply be fertilizer; when having sex, people enthusiastically do all sorts of things that are completely foul in any other context.

So this feeling of nausea about the body is something we learn, and this goes to the core of what we're about as a band. Why is this thing gross and not the other? We've always been curious about things that scare us and gross us out. Maybe that's the difference; when we see these horrible things we don't look away. Why is death from ebola considered worse than, say, cancer, drowning, or poison? All end in death, but hemorrhagic fevers are not a neat and tidy way to go.

Modern society keeps the untidy functions of life compartmentalized. The sick and the old are hidden away from our sight. Sex happens in a bedroom with a locked door. Death is supposed to be invisible in "civilized" society. So is war, homelessness, and the iron hand of the Market. Those things kinda gross us out too, if you must know. And as it turns out, these societal ills go on their merry way precisely because we turn our heads away.

So to the visceral, we turn the same cracked lens we apply to the other things polite society wishes we would stop talking about. These songs are probably not the ones to pull out at a cocktail party or any occasion where food is served.

97

BROKEN BOTTLES

```
A        G       A          G        A
Broken bottles, you've got broken bottles

       G       A                        G
Broken bottles, you have some broken bottles

A                   G          F
Bursting the onions & simmering away

A                    G               F
Let's make a sauce that'll keep them all away

A               G        F
Tender & juicy tomatoes from a can

A                  G                    F
smash them together until there's room inside

             A
The pan for the

      G       A          G        A
Broken bottles; you've got broken bottles

      G       A              G
Broken bottles; I'm selling broken bottles

A                     G              F
Sit back & stare & it shines a bit like grease

A                 G              F
Slump in your chair as we wait for the police

A                G                    F
One will be nice & the other will break your knees

A          G       F     A
Don't reveal to them our recipe

              G       A             G    A
For the broken bottles; you've got broken bottles

      G       A              G
Broken bottles; I have some broken bottles
```

E   B   D   A
I love drugs & I love you

    C   D   F#   B
But I love drugs much more than you

E   B   D   A
You're so smug think you're so great

       C   D   F#   B
Just because you can walk straight

     E   B   D   A
You're a shithead & I'm shitfaced

     C   D   F#   B
Watch me puke on your pillowcase

E   B   D   A
I love drugs & I love you

    C   D   F#   B
But I love drugs much more than you

   E   B   D   A
I yell and roll along the ground

     C   D   F#   B
Drugs will never slap me around

       E   B
Drugs don't call me hippy or punk

    C   D   F#   B
Drugs call me 'potato'

E   B   D   A
I love drugs & I love you

    C   D   F   B
But I love drugs much more than you

E
Drop out of school Yell 'Piss off, mom!'

A   D   E
Rise up and kill your baby sister

E
Fall down, fall down Break your knees

A   D   E
Liver disease brain disease lung disease

E   A   D E   A   D E
Burnt synapses   Burnt synapses

COP KISSER

        A   C
In hot pursuit, ready to shoot
        A   C   G
Lights and sirens blazing
        A   C
Slow it down, turn it around
        A   C   G
What I got for you is amazing
           F
Don't pat me down or read my rights
          E
I've got one thing on my mind tonight

(Chorus)
         A   C   G
I'm a Cop Kisser – Give it right on the lips
  A   C   A#
Cop Kisser – Wanna see your C.H.I.P.S.
  A   C   G
Cop Kisser – Love them boys in blue
         D   E
I'm a Cop Kisser & I wanna go
                        A   C A C G
Downtown with you

With a loaded gun and search light on [A] [C]

I'm hoping you're right behind me [A] [C] [G]

I'm over here and I think it's clear [A] [C]

I want you to do more than fine me [A] [C] [G]

Don't pat me down or read my rights [F]

I've got one thing on my mind tonight [E]

(Chorus)

Turn off the lights, don't need no civilian oversight [Dm] [Am]

Tonight you forget your training [F] [C]

On the BART train, I wanna feel your [Dm]

stick up in my brain [Am]

The pain of your pepper spraying [F] [G]

(Chorus)

IN THE CORN

C
Way back in the corn

       F   C
Between the night and the morn

       F   C
Something died, something born

     G   G7   C
In the corn In the corn

Way back in the corn

       F   C
Between the night and the morn

       F   G   C
Something died, something born in the corn

I am a simple man
But I know everything can be explained
In black and white Euclidean lines
Don't you ever tell me that's gonna change

(Chorus)

The night of that big ol' storm
Took some city folks in from the rain
While Mama cooked, they talked about a book
And said a friend of theirs was waking up again

(Chorus)

They say there's a book that explains
How these shadows could turn into gates
I ain't ever seen a book like that
But I seen how the cat run away

(Chorus)

There's a big ol' light glowing green with desire
That everyone can see from miles away
The weak of heart stagger into my backyard
Drawn in like moths to a flame.

Don't ask me why I killed ma & paw
You'd never believe what I would say
All them folks in them black hooded robes
Telling me I gotta clean my plate

(Chorus)

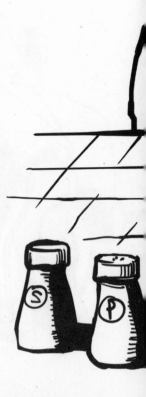

LOST ON A GAMBLER

       G
The cantina went silent

   F   **C**
As the stranger came in from the road

   G
In his eyes I could see

      F   **C**
That he carried a heavy load

   G
Bowlegged like a cowhand

                   Am
But he wasn't a horse-ridin' man

  F   **G**
We all looked away when he asked

           C **(F, C)**
  to use the commode

    G
The old fella rushed

       F   **C**
To the front of the line in great haste

  G
Knocked on the door

 F   **C**
Bowlegged but running in place

  G
'Why did you cut me in line?'

   F   **Am**
Said the lady who now stood behind

   F
He said 'beggin' your pardon

   G   **C** **(F, C)**
But sharting's a special case'

(Chorus)

         F   **C**
Lost on a gambler & falling behind

        G
When ya wager it all that there's

    F   **C** **(F, C)**
  nothing but brown wavy lines

               F
Don't mess with a gambler

               Am   **G**
  when you're out on the town

               F   **G**
Cause your big ol' cojones won't be alone

       F   **C**
  in your chonis when it all comes down

    G   **F**   **C**
Sometimes life hits you below the belt

   G
Sometimes you've got to

     F   **C**
  play the cards that you're dealt

G
Nothin' left but a deuce,

         F   **Am**
  and there ain't no place to cut loose

F   **G**
I'm starting to understand

         C   **(F, C)**
  how the old man felt

(Chorus)

POSTCARDS FROM INFERNO (SEE YOU IN HELL)

You treated us badly, yeah, [F]
  you treated us wrong

So we ran away home and we [A#]

Wrote up this song [C]

And it creeps us out when you don't [F] [A#]

Sing along [C]

You never listened, no, you never cared [F]

You said we were stupid, [A#]

you said we were weird [C]

Well, here's something new [F]

This time you'll be scared [A#] [C]

(Chorus)

We'll see you in Hell, Fun time is over [A#]

No more ice cream, no more four leaf clovers [F] [C]

It's not a party, it's just hot [A#]

& loud 'cause people are crying a lot in Hell [F] [C] [F]

A rock 'n' roll show at the end of the day [F]

Seemed like a chance [A#]

To throw your worries away [C]

Then we came on and screamed about guns [F] [A#] [C]

Life isn't fair and the last thing you need [F]

Is a couple more guys telling you how to be [A#] [C]

But it's no fun for us if you stay on your knees [F] [A#] [C]

(Chorus)

105

IT'S A SMALL WORLD

Bobby Joe Ebola was once hired to perform at a porn industry gala thrown by a lingerie tycoon. The boys were very excited when Heather Kozar (Playmate of the Millenium) & Hugh Hefner began watching their set. In no time at all, the two became visibly disgusted and left.

PINOLE FACTS

Pinole is a sea of fast-food strip malls. With a population of just over 18,000, Pinole has one of the highest per-capita concentrations of fast-food chains anywhere on the west coast.

NEXT TIME, NAME TAGS

G#
Seas of half drank soda cans

F#   E   G#
My cat is lapping beer

G#
A naked man is asleep in glass

F#   E   G#
And how it happened isn't clear

G#
Wet ashes and tortilla chips

F#   E   G#
Are stuck to my grey face

G#
And my throat feels like I drank

F#   E   G#
A gallon full of mace

(Chorus)

F#
And everybody said,

G#   F#
"Is it OK if I sleep on your floor?"

G#
And, "Dude, I'll pay for that hole in the door."

C#   E
My dog was blown up, my house is lost

F#   G#
And it ain't the other way around

Pools of vomit are gathering flies
The cereal's all gone
Taking out the garbage sounds like wind chimes
Someone's bra rests on my bong

The cops showed up at 3
And took the young ones home
Fuck those asshole dickheads
Now there's no one left to bone

(Chorus)

There's pizza in my CD player
Human feces on my porch
A Zippo and a double dare
Now my cock's a phallic torch

The cloud surrounding last night
Is surely bound to fade
But the one thing I remember is
That I did not get laid and everybody said...

(Chorus)

ROCKNROLLFIRE

Take me away
G
rocknroll fire
C
Rock in Hell
G
my rocknroll sire
C
Burn in Hell
F
Burn forever
C
And ever
F
And ever
C
Burn in Hell
G

F# G A Bm C D

Bm
They said I was promising

G
That I was ready to follow

D **A#**
and receive direction

Bm
They didn't look behind my back and

G
see the handle of my knife
protruding from my

D **A#**
pants with which to avoid inspection

Bm **A**
I fought through the effects of all
those drugs

G **Bm**
& made my way across the hall

Bm
'Damned if you'll ever do that to me',
I screamed

G **D** **A#**
& tore the needles from my veins

Bm
I should have stood

It made the wrong impression to be

G **D** **A#**
crawling semiconscious on the tile

F# **G** **A**
I heard his mouth say things like

Bm **C** **D**
'That boy's being sold for dog food'
(repeat)

Bm **A** **G** **Bm**
And I knew he was no dentist

A
His office was just laundering corpses

G
for IAMS and Purina *(Repeat)*

Bm
I broke your fucking drill X-rayed
their severed heads

G **D** **A#**
Now let's see them root canal me
(Repeat)

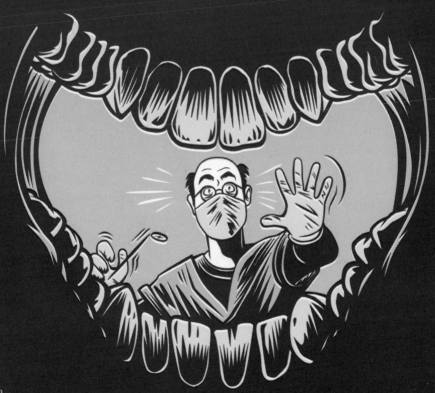

SKIN CANCER

A   D
Everyone's got skin cancer, skin cancer, skin cancer

A
Everyone's got skin cancer

D   A
Who is to blame?

E   A   E   A
Do you get angry? Do you get sad? Do you cry out when they pat you on the back?

D   Dm   A   C
Did you imagine it would come to this? The Sun will burn you to a crisp

E   A
And guess who we can blame?

A   D
Everyone's got skin cancer, skin cancer, skin cancer

A
Everyone's got skin cancer

D   A
Who is to blame?

E   A   E   A
Just take off your clothes and dance around until the radiation puts you in the ground

D   Dm   A   C
Just peel the burnt skin from your flesh, the cockroaches are not impressed

E   A
But you won't hear them complain

A   D
Everyone's got skin cancer, skin cancer, skin cancer

A
Everyone's got skin cancer

D   A
Who is to blame?

E   A
Forget the lotions, deny the creams,

E   A
Just sip your drink and listen to the screams

D   Dm
Just accept that we are out of luck

A   C
That as a whole we all are fucked

E   A
What a blindingly glorious sun

A
Everyone's got skin cancer

D
Skin cancer, skin cancer

A
Everyone's got skin cancer

D   A
Who is to blame?

SLIDING GLASS DOOR

A   E
At the end of the world

D   E
Whose watch was still beating?

A   E
Who was still sleeping

B7   E
And missed the whole thing?

A   E   D
While you were away who crapped

E
on your mistress

D   E
and rolled on your mattress

B7   E
and smeared up the sheets?

C
The dogs didn't do it; They looked

Em
through the window and drooled

C
But this stranger who brings you
   milk every week

G   D
Is doing the things you never let them do

A   E   D
Away in a drawer there's a box

E   A   E
that is covered with old pairs of socks

B7   E
in which hides a gun

A   E   D   E
But it won't be used so it doesn't matter

D   E
She cleaned up the splatters

B7   E
Before you got home

C
The dogs just look in and they know

Em
that the poop that they smell isn't yours

C
They're more hurt 'cause it looks
   like more fun

G   D
to be carelessly pooping inside on the floor

TAKE A PIECE OF ME <small>(THE LEPER)</small>

D A B7 E   A D A

    D   A   B7
The scientists said its spread
   had been dead

    E
New bouts and new

     A   E A
   strains all in my head

   D   A   B7
So I shrugged off the peeling

E
Until I got the feeling

         G   E   A
That my body was falling apart

(Chorus)

    D   A
I'm a leper (There went my ear)

    D   A
I'm a leper (Don't stand so near)

    D   A   G
I'm a leper, so veiled I hurry

E   A
Off to the caves I will scurry

D   A   B7
I lost my job selling hot dogs

     E   A EA
Cause all of my digits were dangling

D   A   B7
I lost my girl, she was my world

     E
She left me when she jerked it off^A
   (jerked it off)

(Chorus)

        D   A   B7
They wrote me a ticket due to my
   sickness

     E   A   EA
They said I was littering limbs

      D   A
They all want a free peek

        B7
At the gross spotted-flesh freak

           E   A
So I'm chargin' a wee fee to see me

(Chorus)

CAMERON FORSLEY 2013

115

THE ONLY DIFFERENCE

E   C#   A   B7   A   B7   E B7
The only difference between you and me is that I'll be awake tomorrow

E   C#   A   B7   A   B7   E
The only problem that I can see is which of your cars I will borrow

B7   E
Will it be the Jaguar? Will it be the Benz?

       A   Am
Be my friend and help me decide

        A   Am
Will the tunnel end in light?

E   C#   A   B7   E   A E
The only night that you have left to live is tonight

        A   Am   E   B7
There's no ideology no pantheon no army you can call upon to save you

E   C# A   B7   A   B7   E   B7
But if it makes you feel less alone, think of what we have in common

E   C#   A   B7   E   A E B7
The only night that you have left to live is tonight

E   C#   A   B7   A   B7   E   B7
Your bank accounts don't mean a thing; I really don't want to hear it

E   C#   A   B7   A   B7   E
Be glad you're duct taped in the trunk and not in your burning condo

B7   E
Will we clear the drawbridge? Will we burn or drown?

E   C#   A   B7
No more possessions, just meat and bones

      A   B7   E
Too beautiful for a coffin

B7   E   A   Am
Whose little candle will sputter first? Let's look into each other's eyes

E   C#   A   B7   E
The only night that we have left to live is tonight

THE SAUSAGE TWIST

G
Albert Einstein failed math

G7
Howard Hughes stopped taking baths

C
Kurt shot smack up every day

A7   D
Pee Wee Herman wacked away

G
George Lucas dropped out early

G7
Larry, Moe, and Curly

C   A7
Jesus got nailed to a tree

Cause simply put folks, Christ couldn't
  dance worth a fuckin' shit

      G
Come on and dance, do the Sausage Twist

     C   G
Come on and dance, you won't be missed

      D C   G   D
If you can't do the Sausage Twist

  G
(Rock rock rock) Yeah you ain't fakin'

  G
(Rock rock rock) Shake your body
  like your bacon

C   G
(Sizzle pop fizzle) Do the Sausage Twist
  (Rock Rock rock)

        D   C   G D
Shake shake shake shake your tiny fist

          G
Come on and dance, do the Sausage Twist

         C   G
Come on and dance you won't be missed

        D C   G   D
If you can't do the Sausage Twist

            G
Just shake your pork, just shake your beef

        C   Cm
Be careful none of it gets caught

       G
 between your teeth

         D C   G
When you're doing the Sausage Twist

ROCK 'N' ROLL TIPS

Going on tour can be an uncomfortable, sleepless, poverty- and diarrhea-inducing experience. Drawing on two decades of accumulated wisdom, we at Bobby Joe Ebola would like to pass on these suggestions for keeping up band morale, if not sanity, on the Endless Road.

NOTHING BUILDS A BAND'S ESPRIT DE CORPS like affectionate nicknames, usually given around 4 a.m. Handles like "Shit-breath," "Chopper," "Truck Stop Buddy," and "Dead Weight," help remind the band that we're all in this together.

THE ROAD IS A LONELY PLACE, and whatever rules you may have at home, they do not apply in the van. Be a sport and give the first round of tour blowjobs. After all, you are in a band, dude. And remember that what goes around, comes around.

SOME FOLKS ARE MORE OUTGOING THAN OTHERS, and that's OK. Help each other make friends! When playing a DIY infoshop or other "safe space," be sure to politely introduce the shyest member of the band as "the former bass player for Skrewdriver."

KEEP A COOLER STOCKED WITH HEALTHY SNACKS LIKE CARROTS. They'll save you money, stave off hunger-induced crankiness, and when bandmates pass out with their shoes on, can be used for all sorts of amusing photo opportunities.

GOTTA TAKE A PISS? PULL OVER! Peeing into a bottle is an excellent way to get pee all over yourself and the van.

POP QUIZ!

Which of these characters do **NOT** appear in a Bobby Joe Ebola song?

A. Bobby the Squirrel

B. Hermie Halbert, the Abrasive Tourette's Fish

C. Santa Claus

D. Smooshie the Turd

E. Kathleen Hanna

F. Bob Dole

G. Glenn Danzig

H. The Kool Aid Man

I. Manute Bol

J. Mr. Turtle

Answers: D, G, I

THIS IS HOW WE GET ANTS

Dm   F
The tyrant is waiting

      C   G
To grant me audience

Dm   F   C   G
Broke her monopoly on violence

        Am   Em
The blanket's a crime scene

F   C
Don't touch the forks and knives

Dm   Em
So many troops on me

    F   G
I almost look alive

(Chorus:)

Am   C   G   C
And I'm dining with the queen

        F   Am
But it looks like Halloween all over me

        C   G   C
Fancy party on the lawn

           F   Am
Til the last morsel is gone party on

    G
Party on

The convoy is marching
   all dressed in black
No mercy, they carry the empire
   on their back
Ironic, I started this picnic
   all alone
Now a litter borne by thousands
   takes her to the throne

(Chorus)

In rooms made of memory, A
   palace for the queen
My heart is a dungeon but you
   won't hear me scream
You don't want to know what's
   going on down south
The whole rotten army can fit
   inside my mouth

(Chorus)

TIME IS CRAWLING

```
EM                  BM      F           EM
SHOVEL ON THE WALL, FILTHY OVERALLS
                    BM              F                       EM
RUSTY-LOOKING STAINS THAT WON'T COME OFF THE FLOOR
                         BM          F          EM
A ROOM OF STEAM AND CHAIN WHERE RELICS ARE CONTAINED
                    BM.    F        EM
UNTIL THE HIDDEN GATE IS OPEN ONCE AGAIN
```

```
        GM      CM        GM                    CM  GM
YOU WERE CHOSEN AND ITS POINTLESS TO EXPLAIN
        CM              GM          CM (B,F,#A,#F)   EM
YOU MAY SCREAM BUT IT'S PROBABLY IN VAIN
              BM      F        EM
AN ALABASTER SPIRE WITHIN A SEA OF RED
              BM  F          EM
FEET ABOVE THE FIRE HANGING BY A THREAD
```

```
              BM                    F              EM
DON'T YOU TRY TO WARN US THERE'S NOTHING YOU CAN DO
                    BM          F            EM
YOUR FEET ARE NOT IMPORTANT BUT WHAT IS LEFT OF YOU
    GM      CM      GM              CM      GM
TIME IS CRAWLING IN A ROOM WITHOUT A VIEW
        CM              GM          CM    A#
DISTANT SCREAMING AND IT SOUNDS LIKE YOU
```

```
                          GM        A#
YOUR DAWNING HORROR AS YOU WAKE
                              GM
THIS WAS NOT JUST A DREAM IT WAS NOT A MISTAKE
                          GM      A#
YOUR DAWNING HORROR AS YOU WAKE
```

A# THIS WAS NOT JUST A DREAM
GM (B F# A# F) EM IT WAS NOT A MISTAKE
BM THE MOONS ARE ALL IN LINE
F EM AND NOW IT IS THE TIME
BM TO REACH OUT WITH OUR HOOKS AND
F EM GIVE TO FOLLOWERS THE SIGN
BM YOU CLAW UP TO THE TOP
F EM THE CLAWING NEVER STOPS
BM SOON YOU'RE NOT ALONE
F EM THE AGE OF MEN IS DONE

DID YOU KNOW?

Dan started out as a journalist in high school, partly because the teacher was quite generous with the hall passes. He went on to write for the East Bay Express, the San Francisco Bay Guardian, and the Alameda Sun, where he worked as associate editor.

Stick It To The Man

WRITERS ~ DAN ABBOTT & CORBETT REDFORD /// EDITOR ~ JASON CHANDLER
CONTRIBUTING ILLUSTRATORS (SEE APPENDIX FOR DETAILS): S. DIVELBISS,
J. KETCHUP, W. SMITH, R. BUCHER, D. EGY, M. CLOTFELTER, M. CLEM, J. NOVAK,
R. C. ROTH-BARREIRO, C. MOORE, P. SORFA, A. DAVIS, C. ROAD, B. PINKEL,
T. CELEMIN, K. MCCARTHY, J. CHANDLER, A. WARNER, D. DAVI, R. Z. RIFFEY

EGGING THE COP CAR WITHIN

We've got a problem with authority. Always have. In that, we're not alone. All of us are lorded over by the multiple intersecting loci of power, known collectively as The Man! The State is the obvious one, of course; they actively parade armed gangs around in a visibly implied threat. But the subtle ways that Money, School, Church, Bosses, Media and Cops (to name just a few) reinforce each other create this oppressive network that makes us as afraid of one power source as any of them. And heck, we play our part, don't we? We police ourselves and each other, and this whole sorry business starts as soon as we can talk to each other, maybe earlier.

There have been times we've flirted with the idea of revolution. Who hasn't? We grew up in the San Francisco Bay Area, a hotbed of all sorts of radicalism, and it certainly made a mark on us. It's tempting to think that we could just storm the Bastille and throw the bums out and usher in a new dawn. But as it turns out, WE'RE the bums we need to throw out. Sure, injustice should be resisted tooth and nail, and yes, civilization is headed over a cliff. But what are you gonna do about the Cop Inside? You can wave all the flags and stockpile all the guns you like, but it won't make you free if you've got a pig looking at you in the mirror every morning.

The songs in this collection are a variety of responses to our interactions with power. Some are us blowing off steam, or complaining, or imagining the logical outcome of what the San Francisco punk band Hickey called the "honkey death culture." In some, we're even trying to come up with solutions that stick it to The Man!

We tend to see revolution as a process rather than an event; you can reshape the world around you in creative ways, making the systems of control obsolete and ineffective. Everyone has the ability to do this. There is no single solution to our problems; there are about seven billion solutions.

🐸 Bobby Joe Ebola Songbook #5 ~ TABLE OF CONTENTS

129

BLUES TURN BROWN

G D C

G
I'm 34, college educated

C   G
and it's hard to find a job

G   Em
Lately I'll do just about anything to

C   D
keep my internet on

C
I just need something in the meantime

G   Em
Because the rent money's almost gone

G   D
So I'm scooping up dog shit

C   D
from my uncle's lawn

(Chorus)

G   C   G   D Em
When the dog shit piles high

C   G   D
It blots out the sky

G   D   C
Until your blues turn brown

G   D   C
And the world slows down

G
I don't deny my privilege

C   G
and I know some have it worse

G
But I'm starting to see

Em   C
how I could shoplift cheese or snatch

D
some old lady's purse

C
I'd like to have a nest egg

G   Em
But my real eggs are almost gone

G   D
So I'm scooping up dog shit

C   D
from my uncle's lawn

(Chorus)

C
I'm in no position to complain

G
You'd only bark me down

C
I'm just trying to pick up

D
what you're putting down

G
It's not my dream vocation,

C   G
it's not what I'd call fun

G   Em
But it's honest pay to be alone all day

C   D
in a backyard in the sun

C   C
I hear the slamming of those doors

G   Em
I'll never knock upon

G   D
And I'm scooping up dog shit

C   D
from my uncle's lawn

(Chorus)

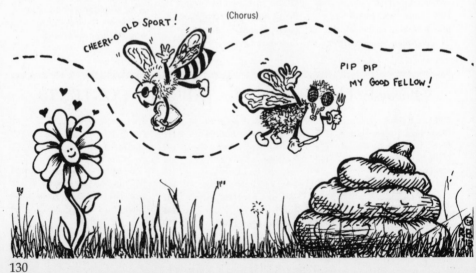

CHEER-O OLD SPORT!

PIP PIP
MY GOOD FELLOW!

E   B7   E
Don't be a jerk at work

      B7   E
No one likes it here to begin with

          E   E7
You are insecure and dumb

            A
You have dragon breath

         Am
Your jokes suck

      E   B7   E
So don't be a jerk at work

    E   B7   E
You're such a jerk at work

           B7   E
I don't care about your weekend

          E
I hope you get hurt

          E7
You have no friends

            A
You're still in the closet

           Am
And you won't come out

E   B7   E
Don't be a jerk at work

I'll give you something

    A
To clean up

                 E
I'll give you something to file

                 A   Am
I'll give you something to write up

  E   B7
I'll pee in your coffee and smile

(Repeat first verse)

        E   B7   E
So, baby, don't be a jerk at work

      B7   E
No one likes it here to begin with

         E
You smell too clean

             E7
You are ruining my day

         A   Am
You stupid jerk

E   B7   E
Don't be a jerk at work

CUHL AIDE MAHN

Dm
I woke up this morning

I looked in the mirror

Through my mind just one
   thought ran

C
As I stared wide-eyed at myself it
   was clear

'Omigod, I'm the Kool Aid Man'

Dm
As I realized this I had to take a
   piss

To the bathroom my feet did
   tread

C
I dropped my pants

Assumed the stance

& damn, my piss was red

Dm
So I stopped to think

I need a drink

Poured myself a cup of me

C
As I took a sip, I began to trip

The drink looked like my pee

Dm
Now I can break through walls

C
I've got big red balls

G   **G7**
Got a glass handle on my side

Dm   **C**
I've got many flavors for you to
   savor

G   **G7**
So c'mon & take a ride

             Dm
I'm the Kool Aid Man

Dm
Now I have a friend

The Great Bluedini

He's a blue octopus with an eight
   foot weenie

C
He swims in the water, & changes
   colors too

from blue to green, then back to

             Dm C G
   then back to blue

             Dm
Now he can break through walls

C
He's got big red balls

G   **G7**
Got a glass handle on his side

             Dm   **C**
He's got many flavors for you
   to savor

132

G   G7
So c'mon & take a ride

          Dm   C G
He's the Kool Aid Man

                   Dm C G
Mahahahahahahan....
(misc. vocal noodling)

         Dm
Now a year's gone by

Still got beady black eyes

& a shock resistance that's poor
          C
My only real gripe is that Tang's
   more liked

G   G7
& I can't fit through no doors

              Dm
Now I can break through walls

           C
I've got big red balls

           G   G7
Got a glass handle on my side

             Dm   C
I've got many flavors for you to
   savor

           G   G7
So c'mon & take a ride

               Dm
I'm the Kool Aid Man

GET OFF MY LAWN

F#   A   B
I got a problem with the neighborhood boys
F#   A   B
Always living it up, always making noise
D   F#
Their balls are ending up where they don't belong
F#   A
And if you won't say who broke my window
B   F#
I'm gonna call your mom

(Chorus)

F#
Get get, get off my lawn
   A   E
You kids get off my lawn
F#
Get get, get off my lawn
   D   E
You kids get off my lawn

F#   A B
I was nappin' I heard them yappin'
F#   A B
I was a veteran, and now I'm wettin' the bed
D   F#
I catch you stealin' and you'll be feelin the pain
F#   A   A   E   B
Go pick out a switch or I'll hit you with my cane, cane, cane
                F#
You'll never do it again

(Chorus)

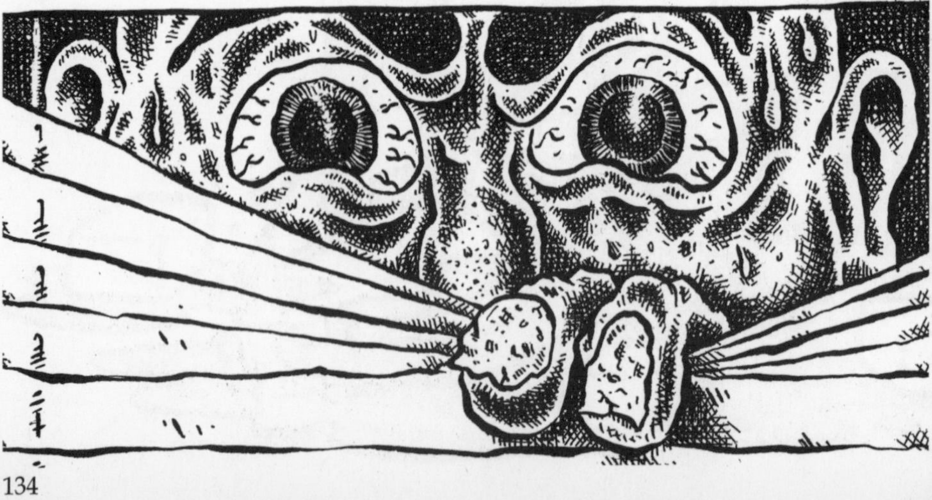

D   A
I called you and I warned you

         C   D#
This time I'm not joking

    D   A   D#
The innards in the alley will be yours

D   A
You can keep my last check

         C   D#
You won't need it where you're going

G   A
Even in Hell they don't make you wear these stupid uniforms

(Chorus)

D   A   C   D#
Hey I've got a bomb and I'm quitting

    D   A   D#
You didn't know who you were shitting on

D   A   C   D#
Think of it as severance pay when this whole place is blown away

G   A   D   A D
Here's my resumé, I've got a bomb

    D   A   C   D#
I told you that one day you would be sorry

     D   A   D#
That one day I'd come back and you'd all bow

D   A   C   D#
Now in my hands I carry your deliverance

          G   A
But you won't be hearing birds sing, you'll hear pow

(Chorus)

135

LIFE IS EXCELLENT

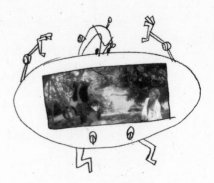

(Chorus)

C   F
Life is excellent

C   F
The tapwater tastes like excrement

Am   C
The skies rain poison

F
but I've got to pay the rent

C   F   C
There's no litter here

F   Am   C
It's only litter where there's no concrete

F   C
It's a rule

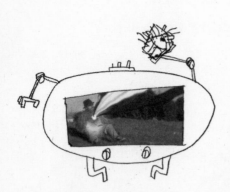

F
Cheesy orange smell

C   F
like cones on the road to hell

Am   C   F
Is it poison? Is it food? Will it sell?

(Chorus)

C   F
I like my glowing box

C   F
and I like my showers hot

Am   C   F
But you can't take the kill out of kilowatt

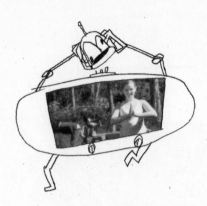

C   F
They've got a lot of gall
C   F
to put a shopping mall
Am   C   F
Where we once had Everything

(Chorus)
C   F   C   F
I wasn't expecting it, but I had to pay the rent
Am C   F   C
Got a job but don't want that job

C   F
I know that talk is cheap
C   F
I know that I am weak

                Am   C   F
But I'd like to be around next week
            Am   C   F
and I don't think there's enough
                 C
plastique for me

(Chorus)

IT'S A SMALL WORLD

In 1999, the band went to Washington, D.C. and visited Congresswoman Patsy Mink (D-HI), aunt of former backup singer John March Mink. While waiting to be seen, they awkwardly shared the lobby with war criminal and former Secretary of State Henry Kissinger, and his small entourage.

In the early 90s, the City of Pinole spent more than $1,000,000 to install dozens of surveillance cameras in its parks, shopping center and around the police station. This had little effect on public safety, but several teenagers were caught smoking pot and carving their initials into park benches.

A storefront at Fitzgerald Plaza featured rows of TV screens showing "The Eyes of Pinole." The city's Orwellian blunder was featured on an episode of the tabloid television show Hard Copy, and the town was nearly forced into bankruptcy.

PAC-MAN & POP TARTS

G# G

C   G
In the land of nothing's free

D#   A#
Where the poor leave home for war

C   G
Most of us see the same two choices

F   G
Too scared to change at all

      C   G
Your eagle hat won't keep you safe

D#   A#
Beanie Babies make poor weapons

C   G   F
Easy Cheese is not good food

             G
So throw away your rations

(Chorus)

      G#   D#
Use it up, wear it out

A#   G#
Make it do or do without

G#   D#
If you still have any doubt

A#   G#
Do you scream when lights go out?

      G#   D#
So buck up, get tough

A#   G#
When survival becomes art

G#   D#
It's not enough to say you will

      A#   G#   G
It's not all Pac-Man and Pop Tarts

      C   G
When you go out, watch for jackals

D#   A#
Do not waste your gasoline

C   G
Make sure that you watch your water

F   G
You don't need to be that clean

C   G
If you discover other people

D#   A#
There are things you must unlearn

      C   G
The flag is stuffed into a bottle

F   G
Now it's time for things to burn

      G#   D#
Use it up, wear it out

A#   G#
Make it do or do without

G#   D#
If you still have any doubt

A#   G#
Do you scream when lights go out?

      G#   D#
It's not the time to stand in line

      A#   G#
The secret cops catch every part

      G#   D#
of anything that moves or speaks

      A#   G#
It's not all Pac-Man and Pop Tarts

      G#   D#
So buck up, get tough

A#   G#
When survival becomes art

G#   D#
It's not enough to say you will

      A#   G#
C
It's not all Pac-Man and Pop Tarts

G   A7
Wiggin' out on No-Doz at 6 am

D   G
Jittery & sick but I'm awake

      Em   Am
This shirt smells like me, too much like me

D
More than I can stand

(Chorus)

        C   G
When I'm low and feeling unimportant

    Em   A
And all my money's gone

C   D
I remember

   G   C
That I know somebody who knows somebody

   D   C
Who brushed past somebody who knows somebody

   G   Em
Who could call somebody who cut off somebody

       C G Em   A
Who could get me in touch with the president

C   D
I am well connected

C   D
I am well connected

C G Em   A   C
O.J. or coffee with that, Mr. President?

C G Em   A   C
O.J. or coffee with that, Mr. President?

      G   A7
The pumps are all self-serve now

        D   G
One less chance for us to meet

Em   Am
I've got a plan; I'll call all my friends

    D
Do I know anybody outside of this town?

(Chorus)

SANDWICHES & AMMUNITION

  A   D   A
Watch out for broken glass & all the obstacles they put into your way

  D   E
To make you feel like you've got nothing better

A
It was a bottle last night

                        D
Filled with some stuff that made the streets

    A   D   E   D
Seem like a playground and the vomit started tasting better

    E   A   D
And in the morning when I tried to ride my bike

  A   D   E
I had to swerve to miss the shards of your attempt to stop the moon from shinin

A
Watch out for your favorite shows, your alarm clock and your paycheck

  D   A   D   E
And all the things they use to keep you greedy and predictable

A
They'll let you out so you can crawl onto a playground

    D   A   D   E   D
where the moon feels like a searchlight & there's no escape or dignity

    E   A   D
And in the morning when I tried to find my bike

         A   D   E
I had to step over the shards of your attempt to stop the moon from shining

A   D
Hey, your hubcaps are flying, there's sirens right behind you

    A   D   E
Your tires squealing as they chase you down for being a hero

A   D
Caltrops are everywhere and snipers try to fuck your day up

         A   D   E   D
'Cause you shot some president and now the TV says you're a bad guy

    E   A   D
Should I believe them or should I root for you

                  A
And take you in like Paul Revere

         D   E   A
And give you sandwiches and ammunition?

SUITCASE

A#   F
With today's technology

      Cm   F   A#
We could build a nuclear bomb and fit it in a suitcase

                F   Cm   F   A#
And whatever you do with it after that would be entirely up to you

                F
With today's technology

      Cm
We could build a nuclear bomb and fit it in a suitcase

                F   A#
And I'm sure you know as well as I where they need to be placed

SWEET SHIT OF CHRIST

G   D
In today's society the church is talked down daily

D   G
So what if priests and small boys are out there having playdates

C   G
Jesus is the reason that war comes around so frequent

                                D   G
What's the fun in life without felonies or villains?

(Chorus)

                  G
Yes, it is true what you heard
      of God and money and of death

                  D
But I'll be singing songs and

                G
      praises until my dying breath

For that Sweet Shit of Christ

Taste everlasting life

D   G
Get your wings and go to paradise

               G
It's been here for some time;
      there's blood on every dime

            D   G
Free wine and wafers everybody get in line

               C
Thought you voted for that one

              G
      with all that common sense

Then come the hail marys,

            D   G
      amens and sacraments

(Chorus)

            G
I am wandering, tired and lonesome

               C   G
Through the pastures and green fields

           G
Lord of Shadows, I am waiting

           D   D7
My soul is empty, let's make a deal

           C   G
Give me power and I'll rejoice

           D   G
The rivers will flow red by and by

           C   G
I will drink from your sweet waters

           D   C   G
& no more will I talk to the sky

THE LAST CHILD SOLDIER

F   A#   F   C
When the last child soldier with the last case of AIDS

    Dm   Am   A#   C
Cuts the last tree down, who will dig his grave?

F   A#   F   C
What did he want it for? Was it for a spear or drum?

    Dm   Am   A#   C   F
Or to build a fire to cook the last cheese dog on?

     A#   F   C
A stack of skulls looming 16 stories high

    Dm   Am   A#   C   F
A penthouse view for the maggots in his eyes

    A#   F   C
It smells real funny and the dead tree gives no shade

    Dm   Am   A# C
And it won't again until we've all decayed

    F   A#   F   C
When the last corporate shill spends the last dollar bill

    Dm   Am A#   C   F
And the viruses can't find anyone to kill

    A#   F   C
What will happen to the plants? Who will feed the pets?

    Dm   Am   A#   C
If there's nobody to jerk off, will there still be internet?

    F   A#   F   C
When the time has come for everyone to die

    Dm   Am   A#   C
Will we have the strength to say goodbye

F   A#   F   C
& in 100 years there will scarcely be a trace

    Dm   Am   A#   C
Of the burst bubble we used to call the human race

    F   A#   F   C
When the last child soldier with the last case of AIDS

    Dm   Am A#   C   F
Cuts the last tree down, who will dig his grave?

    A#   F   C
What did he want it for? Was it for a spear or drum?

    Dm   Am   A# C F
Or to build a fire to cook the last cheese dog on?

      C   F   C   G
You can have the fucking worm, the early bird can kiss my ass
        Am   C
The shining sun does not seem fun
  F   G
I think today I'll pass
      C   F   C   G
I have to say a wasted day is something I regret
        Am   C
But it's my choice to shut out noise,
            F   G
   and spend my time in bed

(*Chorus*)

  F   G   C   F
I close my eyes, there's an amazing show for free
  F   G   C   F
Sheep on swinging stars, singing candy bars
  F   G   F   G
Hot dogs dance with donuts, and a thousand prancing sluts
      C   F   C   G
I'm so not here, I'm not all there, all you heard is sadly true
        Am   C
After last night, I don't feel right
      F   G   C
Waking up is hard to do
  C   F   C   G
Earthquakes and tornadoes could hit this town right now
        Am   C
My bed could lift and start to spin
        F   G
   with cars and trees and cows
  C   F   C   G
None of this would wake me as I soundly sawed some logs
  Am   C   F   G
I'd fall asleep in Oakland and awake in Bogota

(*Chorus*)

THE POOR

E   D
Used to always have a job
A
Back in '93
E   D
You could say those were the salad days
A
And I'd say that I agree
F#   A
After work, I'd get high
E   B
In the backyard with my friends
F#   A
Hit the gravity bong all night long
E   B
Then we'd wake up & work again
B
Now one job is hard to find
A
No way that you'll find two
B
To have enough is way too tough
A   B
So I'm giving up, I'm through...

(Chorus)
E   B
In jail, they serve food
A
The slammer has a roof
C#m   B
In the gutter, there's no P.O. Box
G#   A
They can send your late bills to
E   B
The lizard people own it all
A
And they have their eyes on more
C#m   B
We're gonna die or wear prison stripes
G#   A
You and me, kid; we're the poor

  E   B
  We're the poor
E   B
Maybe it's my own damn fault
A
For not seeking out more knowledge

E   B
But for a welfare kid from a broken
   home
A
Food banks didn't pay for college
F#
Now I hear you yelling,
A   E   B
"Where the hell is my revolution!!"
F#   A
Well, it's paper thin and even if it wins
E   B
It becomes the institution
B
Now I wish I had every penny
A
That I wasted while I was wasted
B
On records with only one good song
A
And all the lovin' I was chasing

(Chorus)
E   B
Cos in jail, they serve food
A
The slammer has a roof
C#m   B
In the gutter, there's no P.O. Box
G#   A
They can send your late bills to
E   B
The lizard people own it all
A
And they have their eyes on more
C#m   B
We're gonna die or wear prison
   stripes
G#   A
You and me, kid; we're the poor
E   B
We're the poor
E B
The poor
  E
So poor

THE ROTTING GAME

    E7
I is so into my anger, I is so into my joy

Either everyone's suicidal or as happy as a box o' toys

    A   E7
Tell me girls, tell me boys

    C#7   F# B7   E   B7
Do you want to save the world or do you want to blow it up?

E7
All I know is things are getting darker

                                          A
All I know is things are things are getting darker, baby

                  E7
The bombs are on their way

        C#7
Send me to the sky

    F#   B7   E
The bombs are on their way

E   Em
Do you have a car? Another way to get around?

      F#m11#5   A   E
Could you leave home in an hour if the bombs were on their way

                        Em
Sometimes I feel like an animal

F#m11#5   A
Caught in the headlights as your fender sends me to the sky

    G   C
I land in a meadow where a thousand bunny rabbits lie

    D   G
Flattened & bloody by the tires of your town

                        C   D
It's like they're watching except their eyes stopped watching anything

                              G
Except the rotting process long ago

    E   Em
You've got a truck and an identity

      F#m11#5   A
I've got my dental records and a tattoo on my arm

    E   Em
All my new friends don't have tattoos anywhere

      F#m11#5
They don't talk much; they don't poop or reproduce or get alarmed

G   C
Maybe 'rabbits' is too strong of a word to use

        D   G
They're more like little furry frisbees rotting in the sun
G   C
I love the games we always play together
        D   G
I lie there decomposing but they're always ahead
    E   Em   F#m11#5   A
My doctor says I need to get some exercise so I don't die
E   Em   F#m11#5   A   G
I keep getting distracted 'cause I'm old & fat & rich & white
             C   D   G
What the hell is coming toward me?
             C   D   G
What the hell is coming toward me?
        E   Em   F#m11#5   A
I've got expensive shoes so people can see me when I run at night
        E   Em   F#m11#5   A
I've got my mylar headband to reflect upon their bright headlights
G   C   D   G
What the hell is coming toward me?
G   C   D   G   Em
What the hell is coming toward me?

ROCK 'N' ROLL TIPS
How to Put Out a Record!

There may come a time when you want to have a recording of your accomplishments. This is an exciting time for a band; an album gives your band an air of permanence and legitimacy. So seriously consider why you want to record. Do you want to get played on the radio? Do you just want something to sell at the merch table?

You're not going to get rich from a self-published album or EP. Even if a label puts out your record, the days of sitting by the pool while the money rolls in are long gone. In a digital world, music is just data. With one CD, theoretically your music could be shared with the entire world for free. The only information you still control is that which cannot be digitized, i.e. the live experience. Recorded music has in some ways become advertisement for the live show.

How much do you want to spend? With today's technology you could record yourself for cheap or free if you know what you're doing, and it is very easy to spend thousands of dollars making a record. Here are a few ways to avoid going broke in the studio:

PRACTICE! – Make sure everyone knows the songs perfectly before recording. Rehearse like crazy in the weeks before you go into the studio.

HAVE A GAME PLAN – Talk with the recording engineer beforehand about the best way to get 'er done on budget. The quickest way is to record everything live, but with this method mistakes are hard to correct.

DON'T GET HIGH – Nothing wastes more studio time than stoned musicians. Some studios will provide you with free pot just to squeeze more hours out of you! Wait to spark up until you're done recording for the day.

LISTEN LATER – After you get a rough mix, the band should listen to the recording several times before you get a final mix. Take notes. Go back into the studio prepared and opinionated.

MASTERING AND DUPLICATION

Mastering, which fine-tunes the highs and lows of the recording and creates a master disk, can get pretty expensive. Studio engineers can do some basic mastering, but radio-level quality takes the skills of a specialist. If you're self-duplicating CDs you can probably skip this step.

Now that you have a master, you can decide how to duplicate your music. Considerations of your band's aesthetics, political philosophy, audience, and other factors will influence what media you use. If you object to the CD, for example, you could put it out on cassette or vinyl. But if you want people to listen to your music as well, consider including a digital download code.

Likewise, consider how you want to present your music. Many stores won't take handmade CDs or releases without barcodes. A mass-produced record carries with it implications of professionalism and legitimacy, but if all your songs are about the evils of industrial capitalism, your medium may want to match the message.

Now that you have your CD, tape, record, wax cylinder, flash drive, or whatever, send it out to your local magazine and wait for the bad reviews to roll in!

POP QUIZ!

What are some other bands Dan and Corbett have been in?

A. The Bob Weirdos

B. Dropkick Murphys

C. Thee Hobo Gobbelins

D. Indigo Girls

E. Iron Ass

F. The Joints of Time

G. Warp Spazm

H. Clan of the Bleeding Eye

I. NSync

J. Neverending Party

K. Blatz

Answers: All are correct except for B, D, I, K.

153

THE TOWN WITH NO BEER

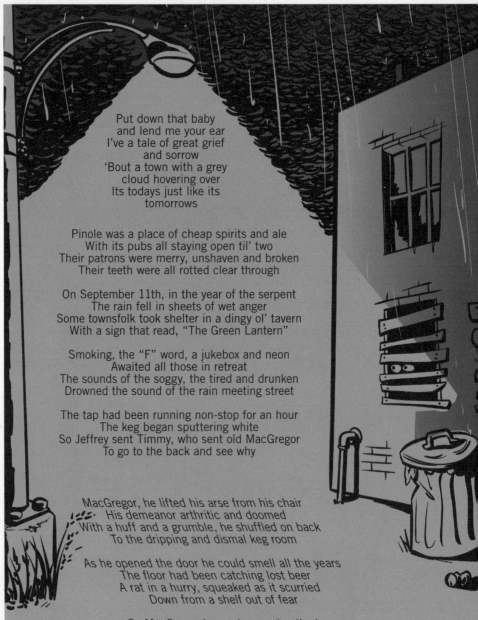

Put down that baby
and lend me your ear
I've a tale of great grief
and sorrow
'Bout a town with a grey
cloud hovering over
Its todays just like its
tomorrows

Pinole was a place of cheap spirits and ale
With its pubs all staying open til' two
Their patrons were merry, unshaven and broken
Their teeth were all rotted clear through

On September 11th, in the year of the serpent
The rain fell in sheets of wet anger
Some townsfolk took shelter in a dingy ol' tavern
With a sign that read, "The Green Lantern"

Smoking, the "F" word, a jukebox and neon
Awaited all those in retreat
The sounds of the soggy, the tired and drunken
Drowned the sound of the rain meeting street

The tap had been running non-stop for an hour
The keg began sputtering white
So Jeffrey sent Timmy, who sent old MacGregor
To go to the back and see why

MacGregor, he lifted his arse from his chair
His demeanor arthritic and doomed
With a huff and a grumble, he shuffled on back
To the dripping and dismal keg room

As he opened the door he could smell all the years
The floor had been catching lost beer
A rat in a hurry, squeaked as it scurried
Down from a shelf out of fear

So MacGregor began to examine the keg
By proceeding to fidget its nozzle
He lifted and pulled the hose end right off
And air hissed out of the spout hole

MacGregor, his eyes, they grew very wide
His mouth started twitching and twisting
He grabbed at his heart with a stiff, quaking hand
And cried out as if he was dying...

"THERE'S NO MORE FUCKING BEER!"

In the town with no beer *(Em)*

The worries are near *(C)*

and the beer truck is stuck in the rain *(D / Em)*

Yes, the worries are near *(Em)*

and we wish they weren't here *(C)*

Cos the worries, they cause us great pain *(D / Em)*

Yes, the worries they cause us great pain *(C / D / Em)*

Yes, the worries they cause us great pain *(C / D / Em)*

Yes, the worries they cause us great pain *(C / D / B / Em)*

155

TWO CATS RUNNING (THE BALLAD OF BOB DOLE)

```
E              A        B7      E
Sex & violence, lesbians, moral depravity
     E              A               B7           E
The girls who dance in nudie booths, for you, and you, and me
     E          A          B7           E
Bob Dole he disapproves of this, he says we'll go to Hell
     E          A      B7           E
But Bobby is no angel, just listen and we'll tell
     E                            A              E
Behind closed doors Bob rips the tie off, prances all around
     E                        A              E
Off with the shirt, then the pants, he throws them on the ground
 A                                        E
Silk panties are so comfortable in his leather chicken suit
    E                           A      B7   E
Whips out the rubber llama and pretends that it is Newt
```

(Chorus:)

```
           A    E    A          E
Yippee-ai ai-yay, be careful what you say
           A    E    A    B7   E
Yippee-ai ai-oh, taking pictures of Bob Dole
```

```
       E                              A          E
Now, Bob, um, aren't  you married? I know there's women down below
     E                        A            E
In the cellar with the peach preserves and shovels for the snow
     E                        A          E
They're tied up and they're screaming "Oh please Bob let us go!"
     E                        A      B7   E
But Bobby takes no notice and sets up the video
```

(Chorus)

```
E                    A     B7
Bobby, what do you have to hide?
E                    A     B7
Bobby, what do you have to hide?
E                    A     B7
Bobby, what do you have to hide?
E              A   B7  E
Bobby, what do you have to hide?
E                            A          E
Tipper Gore and Jesse Helms come over for some tea
     E                            A              E
They listen to some gangster rap and plan their strategy
 A                                      E
They'll pass some laws to keep immoral movies off the shelves
     E                            A      B7   E
Then round them up, drink Spanish Fly and watch 'em by themselves
```

(Chorus)

E
Tarantino and bondage,
cleavage and porno
E
Syringes and corpses and
close shots of cornholes
E   D
J. Edgar Hoover,
G   C
a bulge in his jeans
B7
These are a few of
E
Bob's favorite things

WALK IN THE CROSSWALK

```
         D              A     G#
Walk to the store don't run
       C#m              F#
You can't afford to break your legs
B
You don't really need
              F#
   to see the doctor
       C#m                  F#
Maybe that lump will go away
D
You watched me take
           A        G#
   a 12-hour snooze
 C#m                        F#
I didn't taste the Valium and booze
      B                 F#
The second time around it blocked up
   my tubes
        C#m                    F#
And I looked like a volcano in a pharmacy
 C  G      D        C   G   D
Walk at the crosswalk, look both ways
 C  G  D  C  G  C     A
If you get hit you can't pay
 D                        A
And as they dragged me through
    G#
the antiseptic halls
C#m                     F#
Everyone could smell the puke
      B               F#
They said a credit card was valid ID
      C#m              F#
My pulse just wouldn't do
   C  G  D  C      G   D  A
Walk at the crosswalk, look both ways
 C  G  D  C  G   C     A
If you get hit you can't pay
D               A      G#
I came to just as the orderly
             C#m
Closed the door & walked off
            F#
   to wash his hands
   Bm                    F#
I had a lucky day I survived
            C#m
They know I can't
             F#
   afford to stay alive
 C  G       D
Walk at the crosswalk,
   C  G   D
   look both ways
C  G  D  C
If you get hit
    G   C  A
   you can't pay
```

158

G   C
You are all alone and no one cares about you
D   G
Life is unpleasant and everyone is mean to you
        C   Bm
There's no meaning, there's no god
    Am   G
No objective right or wrong
F
But that's no reason
            D   G
    to kill yourself

YOU DON'T HAVE TO DIE ALONE (C)

TAKE SOMEONE WITH YOU (D)

WHEN YOU GO (G)

BECAUSE THERE ARE BILLIONS (C)

OF PEOPLE (BM)

WHO DON'T KNOW WHAT TO DO (AM / G)

SO WHEN YOU DIE A (F)

VIOLENT DEATH (D)

TAKE THEM WITH YOU (G)

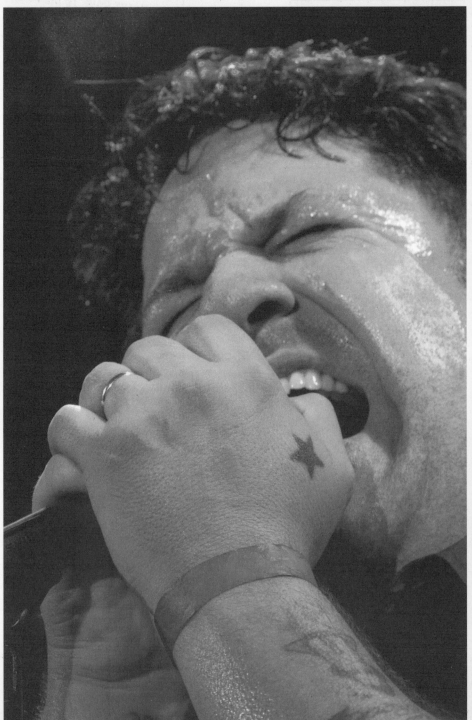

The Bobby Joe Ebola
SONGBOOK #6

WTF Were We Thinking?

DID YOU KNOW?

Corbett had a sketch comedy troupe in high school. Dan wanted to join, but the other troupe members objected to his drug use and overall creepiness. Turns out they had a good point.

IF YOU LOVE YOUR CAR DIE FOR IT.

WTF Were We Thinking?

WRITERS ~ DAN ABBOTT & CORBETT REDFORD /// EDITOR ~ JASON CHANDLER CONTRIBUTING ILLUSTRATORS (SEE APPENDIX FOR DETAILS): M. CLEM, E. WHY, W. SMITH, P. AGUILERA, P. SORFA, M. FOXALL, J. KETCHUP, R.Z. RIFFEY, J. CHANDLER, K. STEIN, J. ISAACSON, J. NOVAK

STAY IN SCHOOL, KIDS!

As you can probably tell by now, being in a band is rarely a well thought-out life choice. Whether sparked by the desire to amplify one's mating songs, or as a means of pissing off the neighbors, or as a source of income, a band can quickly render you unsuitable for any other respectable position in society. Fathers won't want you to date their daughters for long. Employers will chortle at your spotty resume and requests for vacation time. Cops will gleefully pull you over at any opportunity. Critics will either ignore or mercilessly insult you. And all because you decided to pour your heart out in a public forum, the equivalent of reading your diary aloud on a street corner.

This public bloodletting is fulfilling in many ways, but it can also be deeply embarrassing. Anyone who has kept a diary knows that it's a process; not every thought is profound or even correct, not at age 15, nor 18, nor 30.

Look back in your diary and you will likely find a record of petty grievances, clumsy thoughts, and mistaken assumptions, with occasional gems of ageless wisdom. So, too, has been our songwriting process. Some songs that were hilarious to us at age 18 make us wince a little now. For some of our fans, though, those are their favorite songs,

and it's awkward to refuse a request from a 20-year fan, even if he's got fresh barf on his shirt and is being escorted from the venue.

We were teenagers when the band started, and though we had wild imaginations, our range of experiences was limited by our environment. Sometimes we made observations from the sidelines; sometimes we left the game entirely. The songs in this collection represent the odd ducks of our catalogue; the wildest, most disturbing flights of fancy, the esoteric inside jokes that can only come from stoned teenagers, and the stuff we will probably never play live again. You're welcome.

BAKED BEANS & WHISKEY

G
I woke up this morning with nothing to eat

D
& nary a penny to spend

G
I know what I'm having for dinner

C   D   G
It's baked beans and whiskey again

(Chorus)

G
Baked beans & whiskey

D
Baked beans & whiskey I crave

G
And I will eat beans and drink whiskey

C   D   G
Until I am thrown in my grave

If I won the lottery
I tell you now here's what I'd do
I'd buy 99 bottles of whiskey
And I'd give three to you

(Chorus)

Somewhere people are working
Picking beans with their hands
I'd rather shoplift
And eat them straight out of the can

(Chorus)

People tell me drinking
Is gonna kill me someday
But if I die young
I'll never get old & grey

(Chorus)

I like to make trouble and shout a lot
While I still have some breath
I like to shout at the top of my lungs
'Give me whiskey or give me death!'

(Chorus)

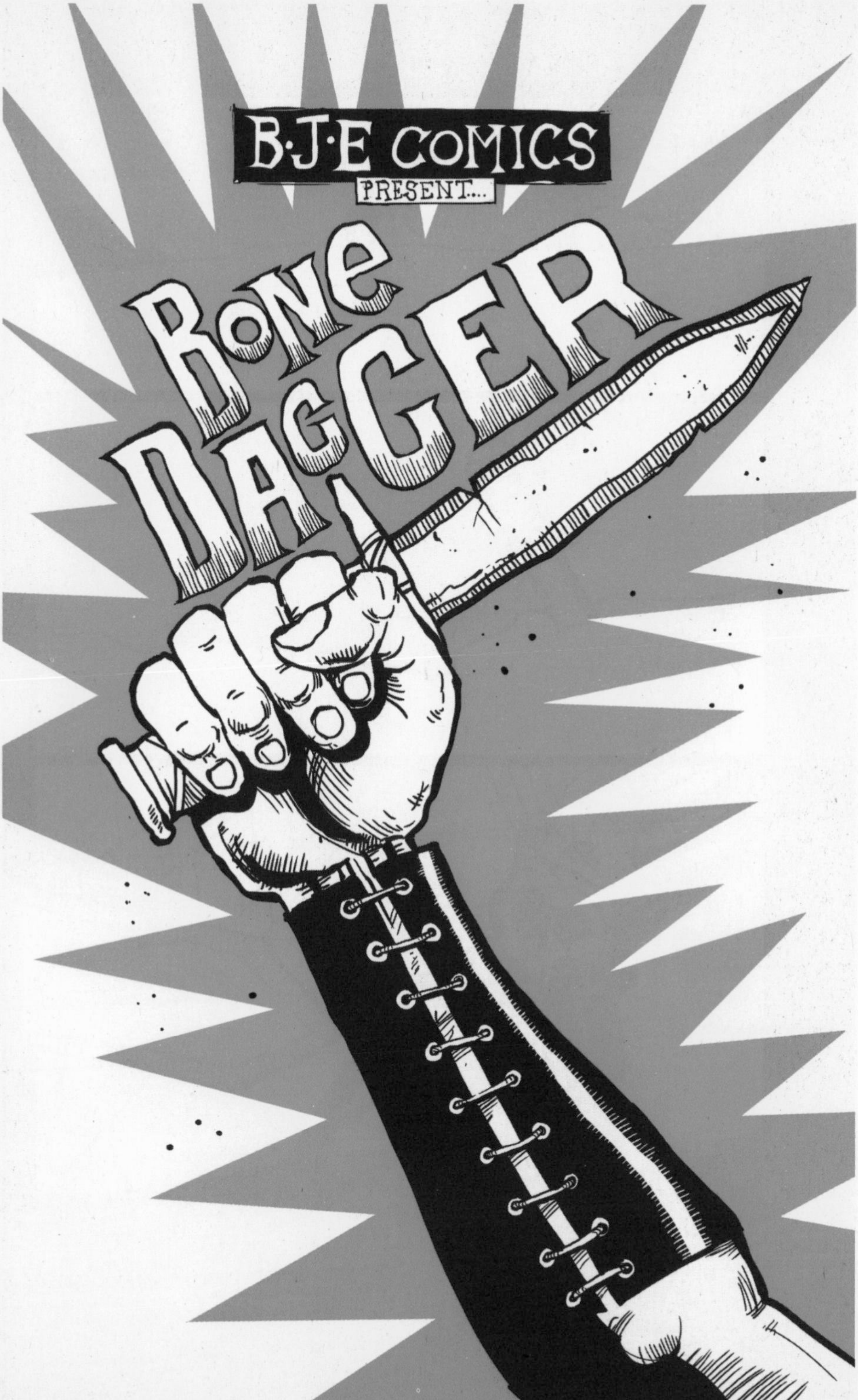
B·J·E COMICS
PRESENT...
BONE DAGGER

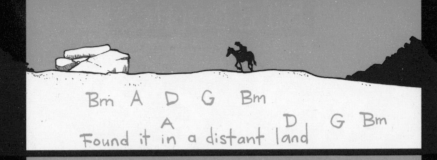

D E E F F♯ B C A B
BONE DAGGER! A Dagger made of BONE!

C A B
I will storm the gates

C A B
I will slice your cakes

C A B
I will jump the moat

C A B D E
I will kiss the goat

168

IT'S A SMALL WORLD

Bobby Joe Ebola was mentioned in *Everybody into the Pool*, a New York Times best-selling collection of short stories by author Beth Lisick. She compared the band's name and sound unfavorably to Ebola Soup, the band her boyfriend "Chicken John" Rinaldi was in at the time.

THE PHILIP K. DICK STORY "PERKY PAT" IS SET IN A POST-NUCLEAR WAR VERSION OF PINOLE.

GIT NEKKID

(Funk jam that just loops around)
F3 no.7, E7 no.5, D9th no.5, C#7
With the occasional measure of
F3 no.7, B, D, C#7

F3 no.7
I said, "C'mon y'all, git nekkid"

Git nekkid just for me

E7 no.5
C'mon y'all git nekkid

D9th no.5   C#7
Git nekkid so I can see

Yo butt, yo booty, a dessert of patootie
Yo ass, yo bottom
Naked cheeks, ya I want 'em
I said, "C'mon y'all, git nekkid"
Git nekkid just for me

There was this hoochie coochie
Her name was LaShawnda
We was havin' sex and "Oops!"
I called her Wanda
She kicked me out of bed and pulled out a gauge
I shoulda been dead from her bloody rage
But I pulled off my condom and I shot it at her face
And got my dope ass right outta that place

I hate Grandmas, yeah, yeah
Yeah, I hate bitches

I said, "C'mon y'all, git nekkid"
Git nekkid just for me
C'mon y'all git nekkid
Git nekkid so I can see...

Yo boobies, yo titties,
  yo knockers, yo melons
Yo body, baby
You should be sellin'

THWIPPPPP

172

I said, "C'mon y'all, git nekkid"
Git nekkid just for me

(For the rest of the song, choose random 80s, 90s
or current pop songs and riff on them to the same
chords. Bobby Joe Ebola has often sang Hall & Oates'
"Maneater", Paula Abdul's "Cold Hearted Snake" and
New Kids On The Block's "Hangin' Tough" during this
"acoustic freestyle" part of the song)

I WISH I WAS SPECIAL

```
D# A# C# G#
 D#                    A#     C# G#          D# A# C# G# D#
I used to have a job, bills, responsibilities

   A#      C#      G#             D#              A#     C# G#
It's so much easier when people think you have a disability

   D#        A#      C#      G#         D# A#  C#    G#
For so long I was so lonely, I thought that no one cared

   D#      A#            C#        G#
Then I got smart and perfected the art

   C# G#     A#
Of acting impaired
```

(Chorus)

```
          C#        G#          C#       G#
Now I sit and drool, go to special schools

          C#           G#           A#
Make sure my words aren't understood

      C#        G#           C#          G#
I get federal grants just for shitting in my pants

      C#       G#     A#
The life of a retard is good
```

← STAGE

174

<pre>
D#   A#   C#   G#
Yesterday Michael Jordan signed my catheter

   D# A#   C# G#
And it made me smile

           D#   A#   C# G#
'Cause I sold it the next day for a Jag

      C#   G#   A#
Now I gimp around in style
</pre>

(Chorus)

<pre>
D#   A#   C#   G#
If I spy a honey that strikes me fly

    D#   A#   C#   G#
I can get away with licking her as she walks by

    D#   A#   C#   G#
And when I go to catch all my favorite bands

    C#   G#   A#
No longer do I have to park in No Man's Land
</pre>

(Chorus)

LAKE OF FLIES

```
Dm                        C
What is the matter with all these flies?

     Dm                   C
And why'd they pick my floor to die?

Dm              C              F            C
Some of them appear to be embedded in the wall

       Dm          C
And maybe it's all in my head

          Dm                      C
But sometimes at night when I'm laying in bed

  Dm                 C              F              C   Dm
I hear these distant chimes and feel like I'm about to fall
```

(Chorus)

```
              G  Am               G  Dm       F          Am        Dm
There's a Lake of Flies where the Host resides in the endless Plane of Worms

                G  Am   G          Dm  F
Where the worlds are thin a rising tide comes in

            Am      G
& with it, other things
```

```
Dm                   C
In the back of a magazine

Dm              C
Next to ads for useless things

Dm              C       F           C
"Psychic readings. Exorcisms. Get your fortunes told."

     Dm            C
She put her hands against the walls

    Dm            C
Her eyes lit up like crystal balls

        Dm           C              F        C   Dm
Then from her mouth I heard a voice both beautiful and old
```

(Chorus)

```
     Dm            C
Now let me see if I have this straight

   Dm                         C
Inside my house there's an invisible gate

     Dm                C        F              C
To a realm that consists of the body of a god that's dead and gone

     Dm        C      Dm          C
& with no other place to go, all of the angels & the crows

   Dm        C          F           C   Dm
Began to feed upon the vast expanse of flesh and bone
```

(Chorus)

ROCK 'N' ROLL TIPS

How to attract groupies.

Everyone knows that the whole point of rock'n'roll is to attract groupies. Groupies, of course, are patrons of the arts who support music with what we might call "physical philanthropy." But often, the music itself is not entirely enough to secure these amorous attentions. Here are a few helpful ways to turn your awkward and depressing singer-songwriter performance into a virtual honeypot for sexual flies of rock'n'roll:

WEAR SUNGLASSES – When your eyes are obscured, it makes people more curious about what lies behind those dark shades. A mysterious countenance makes you seem dangerous and unpredictable, which for some reason is desired in the bedroom.

SEXUAL GYRATIONS – Make your performance a virtual act of public masturbation. No matter the subject of your song, make your performance about doin' it. Writhe into the microphone stand, mime fellatio and cunnilingus on inanimate objects, make sexy hoots and squeals between every lyric, and thrust your crotch back and forth in patron's faces. Things that would get you arrested on the street will be applauded as high art on stage, and will subconsciously implant you in the sexual imaginations of every audience member.

DRUGS – There's something about a drugged up, self-destructive rocker that is considered incredibly attractive. Is it the groupie's maternal instincts kicking in, hoping he/she can nurture the wounded artist with sexual healing? Is it the hope that there might be some more drugs somewhere? Either way, get visibly loaded and watch the groupies swarm in like ants.

TIGHT PANTS – The upside is that you are showing your goods on stage. The downside is that they're a little hard to get out of if you do end up scoring.

ASK FOR SEX – Sometimes it's the squeaky wheel that gets the grease. Don't be afraid to tell the whole audience about your depressing and awkward sex life (or lack thereof). A little bit of sympathy, combined with the above tactics, might just land you a groupie, thereby validating your entire existence as an artist.

WORD JUMBLE!

Unscramble the words to discover what you should pack for tour!

Combine the circled letters in each word to find what Dan almost forgot to bring!

snsrtig _ _ _ _ _ (_) _

wadrruene (_) _ _ _ _ _ _ _ _

spiwe _ (_) _ _ _

laltew _ _ _ _ (_)

pma _ (_) _

hbosohurtt _ _ _ _ _ _ (_) _ _ _

ON KEARNEY

```
      A                        E
On Kearney, there's a hooker for me
          F#m
And I'm sure she'll agree
        E
If I give her a twenty
      A                    E
Don't want no trouble with your pimp
       F#m                      E
I paid you well so don't you call me a gimp
          A                E
Remember that you're a whore
            F#m
Give me some more
        E
It's only cooties
```

(Chorus)

```
Pick it up! Pick it up! Pick it up!
F#m
First street, second street, third street, four
A                        E
Midnight come and me want a good whore
   F#m
Climb on in my Beamer, girl
     A             E            D
Tonight, I'm gonna rock your world
                         A     D
And tomorrow you'll be buried
```

Tomorrow, here's a fifty
I guess I understand
What's that in your hand
and why is is moving?
Cheap slut! What is in my butt?
Feed the bed a quarter and
now you're moving away

(Chorus)

Tomorrow, here's a hundred
And there's the heart shaped spa
Let me have your bra as a
    lacy souvenir
SFPD, you didn't tell me
Now they've replaced that leather
    with cold steel
You squealed; I'll get you in the end
You're the fifth whore
I've been to this week

(Chorus)

APPENDIX

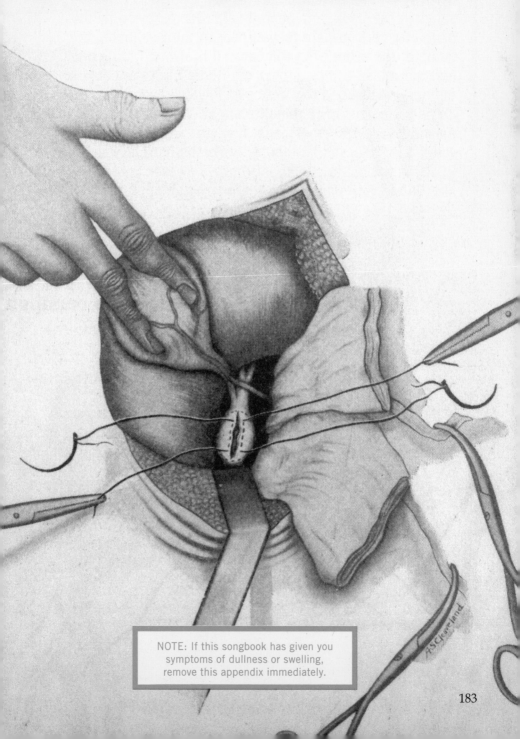

NOTE: If this songbook has given you symptoms of dullness or swelling, remove this appendix immediately.

INDEX OF SONGS & ILLUSTRATIONS

Hi there! Welcome to the appendix, here to help you hunt down your favorite songs! In this list you'll find all the songs in the book, in alphabetical order, followed by the page number(s) where they appear in the Songbook, the name of the artist whose illustrated the song in this book, and the releases they appear on. Some tracks appear on multiple releases; a few are only available as bonus tracks on later versions of **¡Carmelita Sings!: Visions of a Rock Apocalypse**. And some songs, marked "release pending" will not be released by this book's press time, in Fall 2013. If you're curious about those, however, you can likely find live renditions on the internet. Happy hunting!

Jason Novak

Ben Catmull

Suitcase, p. 144; Illustration by: Adam Davis. Appears on: *¡Carmelita Sings!: Visions of a Rock Apocalypse*

Sweet Shit of Christ, p. 145; Illustration by: Cristy Road. Appears on: *F*

Ben Catmull

Take A Piece of Me (The Leper), p. 115; Illustration by: Cameron Forsley. Appears on: *At One With The Dumb*

Tashirojima (The Story Of Cat Island), pp. 58-59; Illustration by: Jennie Cotterill. Appears on: *(release pending)*

The Crazy, pp. 70-71, Illustration by: Arielle Phillips & Jason Chandler. Appears on: *F*

The Dog Ate The Baby, p. 49; Illustration by: Petr Sorfa. Appears on: *Two Cats Running EP*

The Last Child Soldier, p. 146; Illustration by: Petr Sorfa. Appears on: *Trainwreck to Narnia*

The Only Difference, pp. 116-117; Illustration by: Kyle Stein. Photography by: Christopher Poeschle. Appears on: *F*

The Rotting Game, pp. 150-151; Illustration by: Adam Davis. Appears on: *¡Carmelita Sings!: Visions of a Rock Apocalypse*

The Sausage Twist, pp. 118-119; Illustration by: Michael O'Driscoll. Appears on: *At One With The Dumb*

The Town With No Beer, pp. 154-155; Illustration by: Jason Chandler. Appears on: *Meal Deal With The Devil EP*

This Is How We Get Ants, pp. 122-123; Illustration by: Jennie Cotterill Appears. on: *(release pending)*

Time is Crawling, pp. 124-125; Illustration by: Jason Chandler. Photography by: Jamie Dewolf. Appears on: *F*

Two Cats Running (The Ballad of Bob Dole), pp. 156-157; Illustration by: Andy Warner. Appears on: *Two Cats Running EP*

Vanilla American, p. 30; Illustration by: John Isaacson. Appears on: *Trainwreck to Narnia*

Vicarious Fame (I'm Hip), p. 31; Illustration by: Robert Zilla Riffey. Appears on: *¡Carmelita Sings!: Visions of a Rock Apocalypse*

Walk In The Crosswalk, p. 158; Illustration by: Dominic Davi. Appears on: *Trainwreck to Narnia*

Waking Up Is Hard to Do, p. 147; Illustration by: Bill Pinkel. Appears on: *F*

We're Severe, pp. 32-33; Illustration by: Bill Pinkel. Appears on: *At One With The Dumb*

Wryting Love Songs (Will Never Help Me Get the Chycks), pp. 90-91; Illustration by: Max Clotfelter. Appears on: *At One With The Dumb*

You Deprivation Chamber, pp. 92-93; Illustration by: Keeli McCarthy & Jason Chandler. Appears on: *¡Carmelita Sings!: Visions of a Rock Apocalypse*

You Don't Have To Die Alone, p. 159; Illustration by: Robert Zilla Riffey. Appears on: *¡Carmelita Sings!: Visions of a Rock Apocalypse*

JOE EBOLA RELEASES

Two Cats Running EP (CD) - 1996 - S.P.A.M. Records (PUG-001)

We timed the release of our first EP to coincide with the 1996 Presidential election, in the hopes that the title track, "Two Cats Running (The Ballad of Bob Dole)," would become a runaway novelty hit. It didn't happen, but Dr. Demento did play "The Dog Ate The Baby" on his show. We ended up giving away most of these CDs to the kids at Pinole Valley High School. This mostly-acoustic release also marked the beginning of S.P.A.M. Records.

At One With The Dumb (CD) - 1997 - S.P.A.M. Records (PUG-003)

At this point the S.P.A.M. Records crew was living together, starting to put on Geekfest regularly, and as a band we were monstrously prolific. This playful 18-track album is all over the place, as were we. We were still novices with electric band stuff and studio recording, but we had a ton of (stoned) fun. The booklet included lyrics interspersed with a surreal choose-your-own-adventure story. There's stuff on this album we've never once played live.

Advice For Young Lovers (7") - 1998 - S.P.A.M. Records (PUG-007)

The second Geekfest we held, in July 1996, we booked this amazing band called Your Mother. They blew our minds and we immediately recognized them as kindred spirits. After the show we wanted to hang out. "We'd love to," they said, "but half of us are going to see Weird Al tonight. The rest of us are going to see Slayer." We've been friends ever since. This split 7", featuring two tracks from each band, helped cement that sonic bromance.

¡Carmelita Sings!: Visions of a Rock Apocalypse
(CD) - 2000 - S.P.A.M. Records (PUG-015)

At this point in our lives, S.P.A.M. was putting out records for other bands, Geekfest was starting to carve out its own niche in the underground scene, and we were touring like crazy. We were still writing songs at a furious pace, but we were starting to burn out. So we crammed as much as we could onto a CD before the band could break up. A 2007 repress of this, with bonus tracks, was the first release by Thrillhouse Records (THR-001), and a third version, with a booklet of previously unreleased art, was released by Silver Sprocket Bicycle Club in 2011 (SILVER-033).

Freaky Baby EP (digital only) - 2010 - SSBC

While we were in the studio, recording our first new songs in a decade, we somehow ended up writing a rap song. Once that was finished, we simply had to make a rap video, an experience we recommend to anyone. Though it confused and frustrated our label, we found ourselves with a finished EP before the album was ready, and a video for a song that had nothing to do with the album. Helpful advice: when someone asks you if you're a rapper, say yes!

F (LP/CD) - 2010 - SSBC (SILVER 026)

After nearly a decade hiatus, we started playing music and writing together, and this album was that first batch of songs. Our old pal Craigums ran Dutch Oven Studios out of his San Francisco home (the studio has since moved to Oakland), and he was indispensable as a studio engineer, producer, and lead guitarist. We took our time and ended up with a record we actually like to listen to.

Bone Dagger (7") - 2012 - Suckerpunch Records (SPR004)

During a mammoth recording session at Dutch Oven (which produced over 30 songs in a year's time), we started working on "Bone Dagger." The song grew by leaps and bounds before our ears, becoming more and more bombastic. It demanded its own release, and we were powerless to refuse. The amazing artist Mike Foxall got an early copy of the track and came up with a music video, and amazing art for the record. Even though the full album didn't have a home yet, Suckerpunch put out this fun collector's item.

Trainwreck to Narnia
(LP/CD) - 2012 - Rooftop Comedy/Dirt Cult Records (DC054)

After nearly a year in the studio, we had about three albums worth of material, though most of it was earmarked for this or that release elsewhere. We spent a little more time in post-production than with F, making each song on Trainwreck its own album, if that makes any sense. Most of these songs were completely new, but some, like "Censor the Word," had their origins in unfinished songs from the Carmelita period.

Bad Boys Gotta Rock It! (Live Recordings from 1995 – 2013)
(double cassette) - 2013 - Selfish Satan Recordings (SSR #31)

This release was almost 15 years in the making. It was going to be just another album name, but when the band called it quits in 2000, we thought a live album might provide some closure. Life moved on and the project languished for many years, but when we started playing again in 2009, we uncovered some more live tapes. Especially in the early years, the live show was much different than our studio work and this captures the chaos pretty well.

LIVE RECORDINGS FROM 1996 - 2012

Kreamy 'Lectric Santa/Bobby Joe Ebola
(7") - 2013 - Mayfield's All Killer No Filler (MAKNF 001)

This is a collaboration borne out of the network of likeminded weirdos and misfits we found years ago when we first toured through Chattanooga, TN. KLS are longtime freaky art geniuses who, like us, have plied their trade no matter which way the winds of sonic fashion are blowing. The Mayfields have encouraged both bands in word and deed over the years, and this release feels a little bit like pictures from a fun family picnic.

Meal Deal With The Devil
(CD EP/songbook) - 2013 - Microcosm Publishing (THIS IS MICROCOSM 76133)

As little kids, we both used to love our read-along storybooks, and this is an early project finally realized. As early as 1997 we attempted a studio recording of "The Town With No Beer" at KSUN (Sonoma State University's radio station) but the project foundered. After 9/11, we both immediately remembered the first lines, which were just off-the-cuff prose: "On September 11th, in the year of the Serpent/The Rain fell in sheets of wet anger." 2001 was, of course, the Year of the Serpent, which tripped us out a little bit.